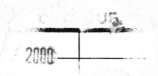
Teaching Martial Arts
The Way of the Master

Teaching Martial Arts
The Way of the Master

by
Sang H. Kim Ph. D.

Turtle Press   Hartford

Library of Congress Card Catalog Number 97-595
ISBN 1-880336-15-4
Second Edition

Photographs by: Luis Correa, Marc Davis, Cynthia Kim, Sang H. Kim, Marc
Yves Regis
Illustrations by: Ken Cotrona
Calligraphy by: Sang H. Kim

To contact the author or order additional copies of this book write:

Turtle Press
401 Silas Deane Hwy.
P.O. Box 290206
Wethersfield, CT 06129-0206
e-mail: sales@turtlepress.com

First Edition   *1991*
Reprinted   *1993*
Reprinted   *1994*
Reprinted   *1995*
Reprinted   *1996*
Second Edition *1997*

Library of Congress Cataloging in Publication Data
Kim, Sang H.
    Teaching martial arts : the way of the master / by Sang H. Kim - - 2nd ed.
        p. cm.
    Rev. ed. of : Teaching. c1991.
    Included index.
    ISBN 1-880336-15-4 (paper)
    1. Martial arts--study and teaching. I. Kim, Sang H. Teaching. II. Title
    GV1101.K55   1997   97-595
    796.8--dc21

Note to Readers

Throughout this book, "he" is used to refer to instructors and students. This is for ease of reading only and should be taken to mean he or she where appropriate.

Acknowledgments

For Jessica,
with love from both of us

For me, "Teaching: The Way of the Master" is a new opening toward a fascinating and challenging journey. Before we begin, I would like to acknowledge those who dedicated their time and shared their valuable ideas with me. For I did not make this journey alone.

This guide has an uncredited co-author. The combination of two minds created, revised and completed it. My co-author is my best friend, partner and love, Cynthia. Whatever faults this book might have, they could have been even worse without her critical sense of editing, her insight and judgement.

I also owe a lot to my teacher, Grandmaster Yong Tak Park who taught me for over two decades and grandmaster Chong Woo Lee who has given me insightful inspiration for this book.

Special appreciation goes to Dr. Un Yong Kim and grandmaster Ho Je Kim for their unceasing encouragement in choosing the right road to the mastery of life and martial arts.

I'm very grateful to my professors, Dr. James Agli, Dr. James Martin, and all the instructors in the Physical Education Department at Southern Connecticut State University.

Special thanks to my student, Dr. Stephen Harrigan of CNN for his skeptical criticism to better this handbook.

Finally, none of this would have been possible without the support of my research by the Master's Alliance. I am indebted to them.

Preface

The second edition of this book is released with additional and updated information for contemporary martial art instructors and future instructors. Thanks to the thousands of comments and suggestions from readers all over the world which have contributed to the revision and improvement of this manual. Many things have changed since 1990, and yet, we are facing the same issues in teaching as we have for decades. Teaching: The Way of the Master has grown into a classic guide to the principles of good teaching and I look forward to many more editions in the future.

The idea for this book was born in the fall of 1979 in a hospital in Korea. While serving in the Korean special forces, I was returning from a mission when my jeep overturned. I was thrown from the jeep and shattered my ankle on a rock. I spent the ensuing months in the hospital reading many books about martial arts and combat strategy. I learned many new things but something was missing. As an instructor, I was very interested in teaching methodology, but I could not find a single book about how to teach martial arts. From that time on, I resolved to study teaching and coaching methodology and some day write a book about my findings.

My hope is that this book will spur others to improve their teaching skills as much as my studies have improved mine. Every instructor should have access to the most updated and scientific knowledge available so we can improve the quality of our teaching beyond the random approach used by so many instructors.

The ideas in this book are based on educational theories and methods from the most classic to the most recent research. They have been tested in the class setting and refined to meet the demands of martial arts teaching. I have omitted much of the theory behind the methods to give you the most direct route to improving your teaching.

My intention for this book is not to be a textbook on teaching, but to be a guidebook. I assume that most instructors already have some background knowledge of martial arts, physiology, anatomy, sports medicine, etc. My goal is to show you how to apply your knowledge in the most effective way based on the concept of *Ji Do*. *Ji* means indicating and *Do* means the way. Teaching martial arts is literally indicating the way for the students. The teacher is a catalyst for learning: an instrument through which knowledge is transmitted. Teaching happens through you, not by you.

View your teaching as an equation - your contribution (knowledge, innovation) plus your students' contributions (skill, effort) equals results (self-improvement for you and your students). The knowledge in this book will help you increase your input into the equation and thereby improve the results.

Read the book chapter by chapter the first time. As you read, some ideas may strike you as highly relevant to your present situation. Note them and add any further ideas you have about that subject. You will find your notes helpful in your daily teaching and you will continue to add new ideas to them each time you reread this book.

The methods for teaching are numerous and varied. In this book, some ideas are very specific and some are general in nature. Because martial arts are comprised of diverse styles, some teaching methods have to be adapted to fit the individual style. Others apply to teaching any subject and can be used easily for every art. Alter the techniques to fit your approach.

In addition to applying established teaching theories to martial arts, I found that martial arts have the unique quality of tradition. Every art has a tradition that must be conveyed by the instructor. So the question becomes, how can we apply these modern teaching methods and still preserve the tradition of the art. My answer is, start with the traditional wisdom of the art. Then, based on traditional principles, apply the best modern methods of teaching and training to improve the quality of the original art. By our innovation and creativity we can keep the martial arts alive and attractive to our modern society. By being open-minded and flexible as well as informed about the foundation of our art, we can lead martial arts into the future.

~ *Sang H. Kim*
  Fox Hill

Contents

The Art

If one is master of one
thing and understands
one thing well, one has at
the same time insight into
and understanding of
many things.

- Vincent Van Gogh

Chapter 1
Martial Arts: An Abstract

Martial Art is the name given to the traditional systems of combat that have been practiced in Eastern and Western civilizations for thousands of years. The origin of martial arts can be found in the need for self-protection. Historically, in every human civilization there has been some threat to personal safety, forcing members of each society to devise a means to protect themselves and their property. Over the years, primitive self-defense skills have been developed and organized into more systematized methods.

Through the systematization of combat skills, ancient warriors began to realize the significant force of the mind in mastering and using their fighting skills. For these early martial artists, combat situations provided an opportunity for self-confrontation and self-discovery. In the midst of the life or death situations that frequently occurred in battle, even one slight miscalculation could lead to death. With death a daily reality, the warriors were forced to hone their skills to perfection.

In their quest for perfection, the most skilled fighters realized the need to be free of fear and to focus on the current moment in the heat of battle. To control their emotions, they attempted to harden themselves through grueling physical training regimens. By pushing their bodies beyond the limits of physical pain, they trained their minds to withstand stress and fear of imminent death. They ultimately discovered that mastery of the body comes through mastery of the mind.

To further understand the relationship of the two, the warriors turned to an inner search for the true potential of the subconscious mind. Through contemplative training, they found the possibility for enlightenment. Enlightenment is the process through which the true meaning of our being is revealed. Through their intense mental and physical training they discovered that in the face of reality nothing is of great significance. The past, the future, how you were, and what you will be, are not of great importance. What you are now is the essence of your life. As they found, every obstacle reveals the solution. It is not the obstacle that we must fear, but it is the mind that hinders the search for a solution.

As society became more civilized, enlightenment became the ultimate goal of martial arts. Martial arts became a way of not only perfecting physical skills, but of uniting the mind and body as one. By understanding the arduous process undertaken centuries ago by the masters, we can enlarge our concept of martial art beyond its usefulness for self-protection. The practice of martial art is a way to a more fulfilling life. It is a path to freedom from self confinement that will lead us to our ultimate goal of total harmony.

Martial Arts direct us to the path to freedom from human limitations.

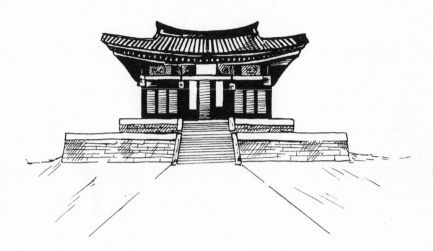

The Tradition of the Martial Arts

Martial art is a system of training the mind, body and spirit to reach the ultimate state of being. Throughout history, humans have sought mental and physical harmony and security. Perhaps this is the reason that many cultures have a unique history of martial arts development that can be traced to the earliest days of their civilization. Organized systems of combat such as French savate, Greek wrestling, Russian Sambo, African tribal war rituals and Brazilian capoiera are all well known examples of martial arts indigenous to one country or culture. Still, it is the Asian countries that have extensively developed the traditional martial arts and introduced them to the modern world. In fact, around the world today, it is the Asian arts of judo, hapkido, karate, kung fu and taekwondo that are most widely practiced.

Many countries have practiced some form of martial arts for thousands of years. But the actual systematization of martial art was influenced greatly when an Indian form of exercise was introduced to China and combined with traditional Chinese movements and Taoism. The moral and spiritual values of Buddhism were also very popular at the time and eventually permeated this system of combat. The combination of fighting skills, Taoism, and Buddhism spread throughout Asia to Northern China, the Philippines, Korea, Japan, Thailand, and Indonesia.

As the interaction between different cultures increased, each country was introduced to the systematized fighting arts of its neighbors and gradually began to incorporate some of these skills into their indigenous fighting systems. In China, the system was combined with traditional movements to create wushu, which is commonly called kung fu. Today there are many styles of kung fu that have been developed from the original art.

In Korea, the combined arts influenced the traditional arts of kwon bup, subak and taekyun and made way for the modern arts of taekwondo and hapkido. In Japan, the Okinawan movements were combined with the Chinese influence to create the system of Okinawate, the predecessor of modern karate. In Thailand, the combination of Buddhism and martial arts formed muay thai and the popular modern sport of Thai boxing.

At the beginning of the twentieth century, these Eastern martial arts began to spread to Europe, North America, South America, and other regions as international access to Asian cultures increased. As the wisdom of the masters and the secret methods of training became more accessible to the Western population, great interest was drawn to the Eastern philosophy and seemingly superhuman abilities associated with martial arts. Gradually, martial arts moved into the mainstream of Western society as an art and as a sport. Just as the integration of Taoism and the martial arts took place fourteen centuries ago in the East, the integration of martial arts and modern educational methods is occurring today in the West.

Techniques

There are countless different cultures on Earth. So too, there are countless systems and styles of martial arts, each with its set of specific techniques. The following is a synopsis of the major categories of techniques found in modern martial arts.

Kicks

Since our legs are longer and more powerful than our arms, kicks are often preferred to hand strikes, especially in the Korean art of taekwondo. The primary kicks used by martial artists are the front kick, side kick, roundhouse kick, back kick, axe kick, whip kick, hook kick, spinning kick, jumping kick, flying kick and multiple kicks. The striking parts of the foot include the heel, side/edge, instep, bottom and ball of the foot as well as the shin. When kicks are executed correctly and with lightening speed, they are some of the most beautiful and powerful techniques in the martial arts.

In close combat, knee kicks such as the straight knee, horizontal knee, vertical knee and drop knee are often used to repel the opponent.

Strikes

The use of the hands is the primary offensive weapon of many styles including karate and tang soo do. Hand strikes include the punch, knife hand strike, ridge hand strike, finger jab, back fist, hammer fist, palm strike and wrist strike. The proper application of body momentum is the key in executing hand techniques. The maximum damage to the opponent is possible when a hand strike is transmitted to one of the opponent's vital points with speed and power. Maximum power is created by using reaction force - twisting the hips, trunk, shoulders, and arms. (see Chapter 4: "The Theory of Power")

Elbow strikes have the brutal power to cause great damage when used to the head. Elbow techniques include the cross elbow, reverse elbow, uppercut, downward elbow and turning elbow strike.

Blocks

A block is a defensive method of cutting off or parrying the opponent's offensive movement using the hands, feet or shin. The primary categories of blocks are low section, middle section, high section and kicking blocks. Blocks are often followed by counter punches, kicks, strikes or throws. Counterattacks can immediately follow the block or can be executed simultaneously. If you are especially fast, the counterattack may precede the blocking motion. Perfect timing and accuracy are critical for successful blocking and counterattacking.

Dodging

Avoiding a blow with a sudden evasive movement is called dodging. Dodging can be divided into two categories: upper body movement and footwork. Examples of upper body dodging are bobbing and weaving, ducking, and twisting away to avoid an incoming attack. Footwork is comprised of many combinations of the following: sliding, stepping, switching stance, spinning, hopping, and skipping. The ideal dodging movement should combine upper body movement and footwork effectively to avoid the attack and create a chance for a counterattack.

Grappling

Grappling is any method of controlling the opponent's movements through direct contact. Grappling often aims to redirect the opponent's offensive force to defeat him with as little resistance as possible. The key in grappling is the effective use of your center of gravity and leverage. The abilities to focus your energy and skillfully control your opponent are very important elements in grappling. Several martial arts have formal systems of grappling techniques including judo, aikido, hapkido, jujitsu and junsado.

Throwing

Throwing, like grappling, capitalizes on the use of your center of gravity. A small person, because of their lower center of gravity, can use throwing techniques to defeat a larger opponent. Against a stronger, more powerful opponent, the impact created by a throw may be much more effective than your blows. The key to effective throwing is to go with the opponent's momentum and use it against him.

Joint Locks

A joint lock is used to immobilize an opponent and can cause severe, permanent damage to the joint against which it is applied. To employ a joint lock, you must force the joint in a direction in which it is not normally meant to move. This is called hyperextension. The most vulnerable parts of the body for joint locks are the neck, shoulder, elbow, wrist, finger, hip and knee.

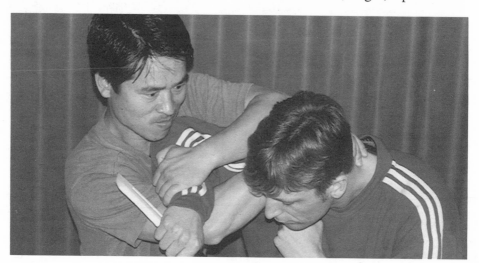

Choking

Choking is a technique used to cut off the air supply to the lungs by pressing on the windpipe of the opponent. It is dangerous to practice this technique without expert supervision, because loss of consciousness can occur within one minute. Another method of choking is to put pressure on the arteries on either side of the neck. This will stop the flow of blood to the brain and can cause loss of consciousness in a matter of seconds.

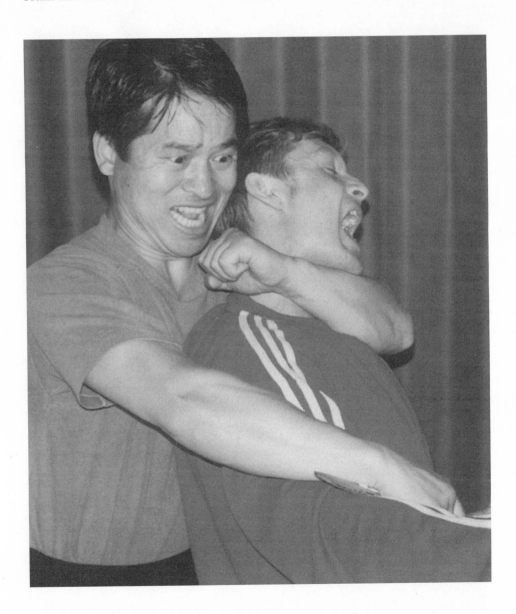

Weapons

Through diligent practice, the average person can develop their hands, feet, knees and elbows into effective tools for self-protection. And the accomplished martial artist, who understands the movement principles of the human body, can hone his limbs into deadly weapons. In addition to physically developing the body, the martial artist must study breath control, posture, and alignment to effectively use his weapons.

Just as the hand is better suited to certain situations than the foot, the stick is sometimes preferable to the sword. Every weapon has its character and purpose. Yet, no matter which weapon you choose, they are all based on the same principle - the weapon is an extension of the body. The internal energy of the practitioner must flow through the weapon. His mind and body must merge with the weapon and take complete control of it. The weapon will become one with him.

When you fully understand how to use a particular weapon, you also will know how to defeat it. By studying its strengths you will find its weakness. This is why it is possible for an unarmed martial artist to defeat an armed attacker. The average person would argue that this takes place only in the movies, and in reality, the armed combatant would always be the victor. Usually this assumption is correct. A skillfully wielded weapon will keep the opponent out of striking range and cause great damage on contact. Add to that the natural psychological intimidation we feel when faced with a knife or stick, and the odds appear to favor the assailant.

But a skilled martial artist, who has thorough knowledge of the weapon he is facing, can penetrate the attacker's zone or knock his weapon away. So, you must understand the limitations of your weapon and be prepared to compensate for them in extreme situations. In practicing with weapons you will find a delicate balance of opposing forces. Advantages vs. disadvantages. Strength vs. weakness. This is why martial arts is a never ending process and even the greatest master is always a student of his art.

Weapons can play an integral part in the advanced martial artist's training.

The Educational Value of Martial Arts

The function of education is to create behavioral changes in a student. If an educative effort does not cause behavioral changes to occur in a student, then it does not have educational value. The result of ongoing education must be concrete and continual changes. More importantly, the changes must be moving in a positive direction. They should be constructive, clear, permanent, healthy changes that help the student progress toward his ultimate goal. They should be beneficial to both the student and to the society to which he belongs.

In this respect, the martial arts have a high educational value. Martial art training has great potential to change a person physically, psychologically and emotionally, in a very positive way. Since martial art training methods are based on natural law, the body can easily adapt to the fundamental techniques and help students reach their top condition.

Once these physical changes begin taking place, they soon lead to the mental and emotional improvements that many people seek through the martial arts. Increased strength, loss of body fat, improved coordination, and perfection of a new skill can all lead to an improved self-image. As the student sees his physical abilities improving, he begins to feel more confident and certain that he can be successful. This leads him to believe in himself, not only in terms of martial arts, but in other areas as well.

This process is especially valuable for children and teenagers. Because young people are beginners at life, they often get lost or confused along the way. This can cause them to feel that they have failed. If they have not learned to deal with failure, they can become involved in a whole variety of self-destructive activities, including drugs and alcohol. If they have experienced and dealt with challenges, such as those presented in learning a martial art, they know that no problem is so great that it cannot be solved. They will take charge of a crisis and dedicate themselves to solving it.

This, of course, is only one of the many valuable lessons children can learn through martial art training. Every instructor has seen many of his students who have improved grades, given up bad habits, found better friends, or in some way changed themselves dramatically because of the martial arts. These changes are all directly linked to the child's improved self-image, and the confidence and maturity that come with it.

Once you have a positive self-image, you no longer need artificial image boosters like drugs, alcohol, gang involvement, criminal activity, or the many other vices available to our young people today. When you feel good about yourself, you can have self-respect. This allows you to accept yourself as you are and to move forward in life even in life-threatening situations. Good self-confidence is the best energizer for self-improvement. When you honestly recognize who you are, and you set your goals, you are on the road to self-growth, success, and happiness.

While this process sounds very logical and progressive, it is actually a difficult road to take. Progress requires hard work, determination and patience. Through the martial arts, children and adults can learn how to handle challenges and how to go forward when they would rather give up. This is the greatest value of martial arts and an education that will last a lifetime.

Function of Martial Arts Training

Physical Changes

Flexibility comes from regular stretching. Over time, stretching tones the muscles and relaxes the body. It enhances circulation reducing stress that otherwise accumulates and destroys the balance in the body.

Agility is the ability to change direction or body position quickly and proceed smoothly with another movement. Agility is a very important that links martial art skills to work together quickly and coherently.

Awareness of the surrounding environment can prevent sudden accidents or external threats from materializing.

Endurance enables you to go the extra mile to achieve your goal. Through regular practice of physical techniques, breathing exercises and good diet both mental and physical stamina improve.

Coordination is the ability to integrate physical and psychological processes into an efficient pattern of movement. Martial arts practice develops coordination by drilling a variety of eye-hand, eye-foot and hand-foot skills.

Accuracy comes from the precise execution of movements by corresponding muscles. Since every technique in martial arts has a particular purpose and target area, accuracy becomes second nature though practice. The habit of accurate execution of techniques brings out an accurate way of thinking in daily decision making.

Power is one of the most critical factors in safety and control. Since martial art applications are, in their purest form, a system of conflict resolution between opposing forces, increased mental and physical power is a natural benefit of training.

Psychological Changes

Confidence is a product of the ability to protect yourself. The intrinsic strength developed in martial art practice affects your daily life by creating a strong sense of self-esteem.

Improved self-image is the result of the positive attitude, knowledge and inner discipline that create a structured method of coping with challenges with a positive attitude.

Certainty that you are in control of yourself and your safety are a common benefit of martial art training.

Belief in success results from succeeding on a regular basis in both the long and short term goals of martial art practice.

The Educational Goals of Martial Arts

In 1956, the White House conference on Education convened in Washington, DC to assemble a list of goals for education of America's school children. The following are those goals which apply to martial arts education:

1. Respect and appreciation for human values and the beliefs of others.

2. Effective work habits and self-discipline.

3. Social competency as a contributing member of family and community.

4. Ethical behavior based on a sense of moral and spiritual values.

5. Intellectual curiosity and eagerness for lifelong learning.

6. Aesthetic appreciation and self-expression in the arts.

7. Mental and physical health.

8. Wise use of time, including constructive leisure pursuits.

9. Understanding for the physical world and man's relationship to it.

10. An awareness of our relationship to the world community.

(U.S. Committee for the White House Conference on Education, 1956)

If martial arts is to be truly valued as a legitimate form of education, we must implement these and other values into the teaching methodology. Let us consider them one by one and see how we can implement them in teaching martial arts.

1. **Respect and appreciation for human values**. Martial arts teaches respect for human values very effectively through a system of etiquette and seniority among students and instructors. Students are taught to respect their instructor and senior students from the first day of class. They learn to bow to their seniors and to respect the spirit of the training hall by bowing when entering and leaving. In addition to respect in the class, they are taught to respect all life and never to use their skill to harm others without cause.

2. **Effective work habits and self-discipline**. Discipline, like respect, is one of the building blocks of martial arts education. Without discipline, a student cannot master the difficult and demanding skills of the arts. To succeed in the class, he must work hard and discipline himself continuously. The instructor can instill discipline in the student by teaching him to set goals and work toward them until he achieves his plan.

3. **Social competency**. Martial arts students are members of an organized society that teaches social responsibility and interaction. In many schools student have responsibilities such as keeping the school clean and caring for equipment. They learn to contribute to their school to make a pleasant and safe atmosphere in which to learn.

4. **Ethical behavior based on moral and spiritual values**. Teaching combat arts to students who do not understand the importance of ethical behavior is very dangerous. Students must understand the correct uses for their knowledge, including what constitutes a self-defense situation in which harming another person is justifiable. A good instructor will make it clear to every student when he is justified in using his knowledge and what amount of force is necessary to protect himself. He will not tolerate attitudes that take the art casually or violently.

5. **Eagerness for lifelong learning**. Martial art is a natural pursuit, well-suited for students of every age and ability. Instructors must consider the needs of students of different age groups when planning curriculum. When he teaches each age group according to their needs, he encourages his students to study the arts throughout their life because they will continue to find new goals and achievements at every level.

6. **Aesthetic appreciation and self-expression in the arts**. In teaching, the instructor should not forget the art in martial art. A good instructor instills in his students both the practical aspects of the art as well as the aesthetic

aspects. Art is highly valued in every society from the most primitive tribesmen to the great Renaissance masters. Every person should cultivate his artistic perspective to develop a well-rounded personality.

7. **Physical and mental health**. Physical and mental health is the most obvious and greatest benefit of martial arts practice. Students feel healthier from the first time they join a class. They learn how to exercise, how to tone their body, how to move naturally, how to improve coordination and much more. A skilled instructor also provides supplementary material like nutritional information, exercise guidelines, and weight training programs to increase his students' health even further. As their physical health improves, students begin to feel better about themselves. They gain more confidence in their physical being, have less stress and feel at ease with themselves. This can surely be defined as mentally healthy.

8. **Wise use of time including constructive leisure pursuits**. A martial art is an excellent leisure pursuit and is becoming recognized throughout the world as such. It encourages a healthy life-style and a sound mind. It also teaches students how to manage their time by introducing the concept of setting and achieving goals regularly. Most martial arts can be practiced by all ages and are a good activity for families to participate in together.

9. **Understanding the physical world and man's relationship to it**. Martial art is based on natural movements. It has been derived from in depth study of the human body and the principles of nature. The student can be taught about his relationship to the world around him through explanations of natural phenomena and how they relate to training. For example, consider the power and suppleness of water or the strength and flexibility of bamboo.

10. **An awareness of our relationship to the world community**. Martial art is practiced throughout the world. By encouraging students to meet and exchange ideas with each other on a global scale, such as international seminars and competition, we are encouraging the development of a truly global community.

Beyond these goals of mainstream education, the martial arts have goals that are unique. They include perfection of skills, self-fulfillment though self-improvement and betterment of the art. So, we can summarize the goals of martial art as follows:

Physical goals:

1. Perfection of skills
2. Physical and mental health
3. Betterment of the art
4. Understanding the physical world and man's relationships to it

Intellectual goals:

1. Effective work habits and self-discipline
2. Social competency
3. Eagerness for lifelong learning
4. Wise use of time
5. An awareness of our relationship to the world community

Value-oriented goals:

1. Respect and appreciation for human values
2. Ethical behavior
3. Aesthetic appreciation and self-expression through the art
4. Self-fulfillment through self-improvement

With specific, proven goals such as these, a professional instructor can feel confident presenting his program to schools, recreation programs, parents and potential students. Based on thorough, scientific research, these goals of martial art education are parallel to the goals of mainstream education, making them more appealing to educators than the vague benefits of "confidence, self-esteem, etc." that are normally touted by martial art programs. By speaking the language of the educational community, the instructor can create a professional image.

However, many of these goals are abstract and long-term in nature, so teaching must be oriented toward more than learning physical skills. A competent instructor must be a person who can understand and communicate moral values and human relationships as well as teach physical skills effectively to fulfill his goals.

Teaching

What is more malleable is always superior over that which is immovable. This is the principle of controlling things by going along with them, of mastery through adaptation.

— Lao Tzu

Chapter 2

The Essence of Teaching

Teaching is a means of imparting knowledge through specific lessons. A teacher of martial art is a specialist who guides his or her students through the development of specific physical and mental skills. A teacher must be a person who is an expert in the subject he teaches. In the field of martial arts, this expertise should be based on solid professional knowledge and experience in the arts being taught.

Teaching is an integral part of the martial arts. Without good teachers, there can be no future for the art. The spirit of the martial arts prospers through student-teacher relationships. It is the passing of knowledge from one generation of martial artists to the next that gives the martial arts its rich history and culture. For serious martial artists, the teacher-student bond is highly respected.

When a student reaches a level at which he is qualified to teach, he often truly recognizes for the first time, how talented his teacher is. He realizes that being a good fighter or martial arts practitioner does not automatically mean you can be a good teacher. Without a certain degree of experience in all areas of the martial arts, it is difficult to teach. An instructor must be well-rounded and experienced in as many facets of his art as possible since martial art contains an unfathomable amount of wisdom and knowledge that you must experience directly to understand.

If you flip through the ads for your local martial arts schools you might get the impression that being some kind of champion is a prerequisite for being an instructor. In reality, what you are is more important than what you have done in the past. To be a good instructor you have to do more than teach. You have to understand and relate to your students. You must have a sense of mission and motivation for what you are doing. You must have knowledge and experience as well as a sense of professionalism. Above all, you have to believe in what you are doing.

Teaching martial arts involves giving others the knowledge required to perform specific physical movements and sharing the spirit of your art with them. Unfortunately, there is not a secret method or trick that can make an instructor instantly successful. Your teaching method is largely determined by your style, character, cultural heritage, personality and martial arts background. This means that there can be as many different teaching methods as there are teachers. Still there are fundamental formulas that you can apply to your teaching style to make it as effective as possible.

5 Principles of Teaching

1. Planning

The foremost element in teaching is careful planning. Plan the objectives for each class and delegate the amount of practice time you will allow for each. For effectiveness and safety, carefully consider the type and number of exercises and skills you will teach in every class.

Set goals for each class. Students can perform better and learn more quickly when they have goals to work toward. In setting your classroom goals, it is best to identify each individual's strengths and weaknesses whenever possible. This insures smooth progress and avoids unnecessary frustration. For the greatest motivational value, goals must be specific and reasonably difficult to accomplish. (For a more detailed discussion of planning, see Chapter 5)

2. Motivation

It will make your job easier and more successful when you have students who are motivated to learn. The desire to change and acquire new skills is necessary for a student to continue studying martial arts for a long period of time. The single best way to motivate others is to be a highly motivated person yourself. (For a more detailed discussion of motivation, see CH. 3)

3. Recognition of Individuality

Every individual has a different way of perceiving and understanding the world around him. Since you are teaching a group of individuals you must consider every person individually and as a part of the whole. Every individual learns at his own pace and to the best of his ability. Inherent to being a good instructor is the aptitude for teaching the class as a unified whole while giving each individual the specific instruction he needs to improve.

You must master the ability to balance the need for individuality with the need for conformity. While there are many things that all students perform uniformly, an overemphasis on conformity can stifle a student's natural talent. Because we are all unique persons with unique physical and mental characteristics, we each have special talents and weaknesses. By accurately recognizing these strengths and weaknesses, we can maximize our potential. We are both confined and compelled by our uniqueness.

Yet, within the martial arts there is a special tradition and heritage that have been handed down to us. It is our duty to preserve the character of our art and to pass it on to our students. Therefore, we require that students practice certain skills in a specifically designated way, without digression. A good example of this is the practice of forms. Every white belt in a particular style practices the same form in the same way that every white belt before him practiced it. This is a way of preserving the tradition of our art. Of course some people kick higher or punch faster than others, but this does not mean that to showcase the kickers we demand that everyone kick high or to accommodate the punchers, we substitute punches for kicks. This would be time consuming and detrimental to the martial arts as a whole. To teach effectively we must set the standards for students as well as encourage their individuality.

4. Practice

Regardless of their individual needs and differences, all students need the opportunity to practice what they have learned. Repetition is the best method of practice to perfect a skill. Supervise your students' practice sessions whenever possible. This will prevent them from practicing flawed techniques that could lead to bad habits or injuries. When a student reaches the advanced level, practice becomes even more important because of the broad scope and difficulty of techniques being learned. Many advanced students tend to stop practicing basic techniques. Remind them to continue to keep their foundation strong. Every good instructor recognizes that fundamental skills are prerequisite to success in the martial arts.

In addition to regularly scheduled classes and supervised practice sessions, many students may need specific guidelines for their personal practice sessions. For tournament competitors, for example, two or three classes per week are not enough. At least five or six periods per week must be spent in a well planned and consistent practice program. If a competitor practices three times a week in the school, he should practice two or three times by himself. His additional practice sessions might include things not fully covered in class such as interval training, stamina work, short and long distance running, speed training, weight training, etc.

A practice program should be planned with diversity. The program must include training for power, speed, endurance, strength, flexibility, and reflexes. It is best to train one day concentrating on physical intensity and next day with emphasis on mental skills such as accuracy, reflexes or strategy.

When a beginner must practice alone, let him practice with emphasis on slow, correctly performed techniques. He should not have anxiety over mastering techniques overnight or with great speed. More beginners get injured when they practice alone than when they practice in class. The reasons for this are improper warm-up, incorrect execution of movements, and overanxiety.

The best way to prevent injuries and setbacks is to practice under a qualified instructor's supervision. With an instructor's guidance, students can maximize their power and speed so that they can break through their present limitations and move on to the next level of skills. If a student experiences a plateau in his training help him overcome it by reassuring him that it is a normal step on the path of learning. You also can provide him with alternative practice methods such as meditation, traditional conditioning exercises or reading materials that may give him insight into his situation.

Practicing is the road to mastery. There are many paths to take. Some are uphill, some are downhill, and some are long flat stretches of smooth sailing. As an instructor you have to be able to visualize the entire path for every one of your students. When a student is progressing well, let him go along by himself. When he is struggling uphill, gently push him higher. When he is rushing downhill, give him your hands to slow his ride.

Be creative in motivating your students to continue practicing. If you make them consistent in their practice, they will reach the destination they dreamed of on the first day of class. (For a more detailed discussion of practice, see Chapter 3)

5. Performance Assessment

Performance Assessment is a data collection process that is used to comprehensively check a student's progress and correct errors in his performance. It is an essential technique that should be used daily by all instructors. Performance Assessment has four progressive steps: (1) Appraisal and Analysis, (2) Feedback, (3) Reinforcement and (4) Follow-up. Once you begin using this process to check your students' performance, you will find that the four steps follow each other naturally and that you use them constantly in your teaching.

The first step in Performance Assessment is **Appraisal and Analysis**. This is actually two separate but related steps. Appraisal takes place when you watch an individual student's performance and determine his current skill level. In doing this, note his general condition and improvements made since his last Performance Assessment. If a student is performing a specific movement incorrectly or that he generally has a bad habit, analyze exactly where the difficulty lies. Accurate analysis is very important because if you incorrectly diagnose the problem, the student will continue to perform poorly.

Step two is **Feedback**. Feedback simply means telling the student how he is progressing. In learning a new skill, a student cannot accurately judge if he is executing it properly. Guide him toward the correct movement through verbal and physical reminders. Correct a mistake as soon as it occurs to prevent it from becoming habitual. If the error does become a habit it can still be corrected through consistent feedback. Using negative feedback for incorrect actions and positive feedback for correct actions will considerably accelerate student learning.

Feedback must be followed by **Reinforcement**. For some students, the enjoyment of performing well can be enough reinforcement to make them continue to improve. But even highly motivated students occasionally need some kind of external reinforcement. Reinforcement is similar to feedback, in the sense that there are two types of reinforcement you can employ - negative and positive. Positive reinforcement includes individual praise or, less frequently, a material reward for desired behavior.

Negative reinforcement means ignoring or discouraging undesirable behavior. In extreme situations, especially when the safety of other students is at risk, punishment may be required. Only use negative reinforcement or punishment only when a person fails to respond to positive techniques. Unlike positive guidance, negative reinforcement discourages the student's undesirable behavior, but it fails to provide him with an alternative behavior.

The final step of Performance Assessment is **Follow-up**. Check each student's progress regularly with particular attention to his or her previous difficulties. Follow-up is used to ensure that the student can and is performing in the way that he was taught. It also prevents the student from slipping back into bad habits that could result in a loss of effectiveness in his training.

These principles of teaching are the fundamental elements in creating a favorable learning environment. Their successful implementation is dependent on the skill of the teacher. As you plan your curriculum, consider each subject from the viewpoint of each of the above principles:

How will I plan this subject?
How will I motivate students to be interested in it?
How can my students practice this new skill for maximum effectiveness?
How much freedom should I allow students in altering this skill to fit their individual needs?
How will I assess the correctness of the students' performance of this new skill?

Use these five questions when planning your curriculum. They will keep your teaching fresh and well organized indefinitely.

Performance Assessment

1. Appraisal and Analysis
2. Feedback
   · positive
   · negative
3. Reinforcement
   · positive
   · negative
4. Follow-up

Attributes

All know the way; few actually walk it.

— Bodhidarma

CHAPTER 3
Attributes of a Martial Artist

To provide your students with the best possible learning experience, it is necessary for you to improve what you are doing on a daily, weekly, monthly and yearly basis. If you are always improving your teaching methods, your students will continue to enjoy learning in your school indefinitely. Be enthusiastic about your job. Set the priorities for your class and stick to them. Motivate yourself with the same positive mentality that you use for your students.

In this chapter are what I believe to be the primary qualities of a true martial artist. With discipline, respect, motivation, a positive attitude, and lots of practice, a martial artist can master any task and conquer any challenge. When you read this chapter, consider how to instill these attributes in your students.

Motivation

Motivation is the mental spark that energizes a person for action. To move your body, you must first move your mind. To move your mind, you must be aroused by an internal or external stimulus. This powerful stimulus is known as motivation. In a teaching environment, the stimulus may be different for each individual or it may be the common factor in a group activity. To motivate your students, first discover what mental or emotional stimuli lie behind their desire to learn.

Students must be motivated if they want to achieve the superior performance levels and psychological rewards that martial arts can offer. If they are not motivated, their training will become mechanical and their performance will be poor. If you motivate them well, they will feel that their ability to progress is limitless. In motivation, as in discipline, student behavior is directly related to the behavior of their instructor. If you are highly motivated, your attitude will energize your student's actions and guide them toward their goal.

So we can conclude that motivated behavior is the result of the presence of proper student arousal and a goal oriented atmosphere created by the instructor. There are many ways to motivate students according to the preference and character of the instructor. Through my experience, I have found that there are a few simple principles that can motivate students in any teaching situation.

1. Never hesitate to **encourage or praise students** when they perform well (The emphasis here is on "when they perform well". Overuse of praise can make students dependent and discourage intrinsic motivation)

2. Always encourage students to **try again** when they have made a mistake or experienced failure. A process of trial and error is necessary to produce anything worthwhile.

3. When setting goals, **clearly state what the goal is**, how to proceed, and how the student will know when he or she has reached the goal.

4. **Present new tasks in small, easy to master steps**.
   Learning progresses smoothly and intrinsic motivation is
   heightened when success is the result of reasonable effort.

5. **Failure is the predecessor to success**. Without first
   failing, we cannot succeed.

Although failure does not initially sound like a motivating force, it can be if it is used correctly. Failure leads to a decrease in motivation only when it is accepted as failure. Failure leads students to improve when they see it is a stepping stone on the road to success. It then becomes part of the process of growing up and finding a way to perfection. Once students overcome failure, it will give them the inner strength that they need to improve, sustain and master a technique.

You also can motivate students by creating a system of rewards and incentives. Material rewards include medals, awards, trophies, and rank promotions. If you promote unqualified students or make trophies the goal of training, your students will eventually lose interest because you are devaluing their hard work. But encouraging healthy competition among class members and entering students in tournaments are effective motivational techniques as long as competitors are equally matched in ability and skill level.

It is also important to provide nonmaterial means of motivation. Simply giving students good advice about their training at the right time can keep them on the right track. Verbal incentives and encouragement in the class setting are particularly effective because the student feels that he has achieved something worthy of recognition by his instructor.

When a student reaches a designated goal, help him establish a new one immediately. Ongoing goals encourage students to increase their efforts. Goals should be well suited to the student's ability but challenging. This way, when they reach their goal, they will have increased their self-esteem and social standing in the class.

Though you set clear goals and provide adequate incentives and encouragement, there will always be students who don't respond. Perhaps you will find the reason for their lack of motivation in the following paragraphs where typical problems are followed by suggested solution.

Boring subject

Present the subject in an interesting, new, unusual, or exciting way. Use drills, games, variations and applications to distract the students from the inherent monotony of the subject.

Great effort required

Break large, long-term or difficult skills into smaller segmented tasks and provide rewards for meeting short term goals. Remind the student of the reward that will result from pursuing a difficult task. In general, complex tasks result in highly rewarding accomplishments. Encourage the student to have endurance and present the task as a way to develop discipline.

Doesn't understand concept

Explain the subject clearly or try explaining from a different reference point. Demonstrate the skill according to student's ability level, slower and in parts for beginners. Relate the skill to a skill the student already understands well.

Lack of ability

Simplify tasks to bring them to a realistic level for the student. Allow the student to have more time to practice or develop the necessary fitness level. Give the student individual help outside of class or assign an assistant instructor to work with him or her privately.

Student is tired

Delay teaching new or complex skills until next class. Review previously learned material and emphasize a relaxed performance. Allow the student time for meditation before class to rejuvenate the mind.

Student is scared, insecure

Ensure that classroom safety is adequate. Review the rules with students and emphasize the reasons behind the rules. Use protection gear in activities where accidental contact might occur. Control range and freedom of skills in use to those appropriate for the students' skill level. Pair insecure students with sympathetic partners who will use good control and demonstrate a cooperative attitude.

Student has low esteem

Reassure of the student of his ability. Praise small achievements, but always find areas of real improvement. False praise can further damages the student's self-image. Be positive when dealing with the student.

Fear of failure

Present occasional safe risk opportunities during the class. Start with easy to master situations and work up to confronting the student's fear. Control the class environment to prevent failure by use of group and team activities.

Student dependent on instructor praise

Encourage the student to set his own goals and reward himself when reaching them. Reduce the frequency of praise from the instructor and provide opportunities for the student to gain fulfillment from doing well. Direct the student toward the intrinsic rewards of performing well and improving. Suggest the student log his achievements in a personal training diary.

No matter what method you choose to motivate your students, remember that you are being observed by your students. Your behavior will be followed as that of a model martial artist. This is especially true of young students. Teach by example and your students will respect you for it. Before being an instructor, know how to be a good student who is strongly motivated to work hard and honest enough to be humble in the pursuit of mastery.

Positive Attitude

In teaching you can never overemphasize the importance of a positive attitude. If you allow your students to approach learning with a closed mind or a negative attitude then a negative atmosphere will prevail in your school. This can quickly destroy the effects of your teaching and discourage even the most optimistic students. Teach your students that in human nature the positive always defeats the negative.

Many people who join your school already understand this and have a strong determination to learn martial arts. These people will make your job easy. But there also will be those who join your class for other reasons. Some people join out of curiosity. Some have a fantasy of becoming a master overnight. Some people are talked into joining by their parents or friends. And some people even join out of necessity; they feel they must learn self-defense to survive in today's crime ridden society.

Though they appear to be ready to learn, they may find the reality of training hard to accept. The school rules and the conduct of the other students are foreign to them and they may have difficulty following along. Your ability to instill in them a positive attitude will make their martial arts experience enjoyable and will determine how long they continue to learn.

One of the simplest ways to instill a positive attitude in the beginner student is to use a comparative approach. For example, would he rather be lazy or diligent, weak or strong, awkward or coordinated? Ultimately, does he want to give a poor or perfect performance? These comparisons provide him with a clear image of what he can accomplish through training. If the student confidently chooses the correct answers, then he has already started on the road to a positive attitude.

At first this student will progress quickly because of his desire to learn. There will, however, come a time when relatively little improvement is taking place. The student has reached a certain skill level and appears to be stuck there. This is called a plateau. **Plateaus** often occur when training under conditions of prolonged fatigue, personal difficulty, or due to changes in the learning environment. For intermediate students, a plateau can occur when the student attempts to learn complex skills without the proper physical preparation or knowledge.

When you notice that someone has reached a plateau, show him how to overcome it with a positive attitude. If he is having difficulty performing a specific movement, break it into segments and teach it slowly and correctly. Encourage him to return to more basics to build confidence. Through practice and patience he will find a way to break through to the next level of learning.

If the student is afraid of learning new skills or afraid of failure, help him overcome this by using a positive approach. The mind is the master of the body. If he concentrates on his fear he will be paralyzed by it. If he thinks only of failure, he will fail. When he thinks of success, he will succeed. If he concentrates on happiness he will be happy. The happiness and enlightenment sought through martial arts for centuries can only be attained by arming the mind with a positive outlook.

When you have an optimistic view of life, it will inevitably affect the people you teach. In fact, the positive attitude your students develop will spill over into other areas of their life as well. By teaching them to approach their problems with an indomitable spirit, you are giving them the dynamic energy they need to overcome the obstacles that stand between them and their goals in life.

The positive always defeats the negative.

Physical Practice

Martial arts is an active philosophy. It is a way to express your aesthetic potential through physical movement. The key phrase is physical movement, because in the martial arts, as in all else, practice makes perfect.

The value of consistent practice can never overemphasized. When students have learned a particular technique, accentuate the importance of devoted practice. But before they practice, students must know what to do and how to do it. Teach them the goal of the movement and the means by which they can accomplish that goal. In other words, instill in the students' minds a perfect image of the movement you want them to learn. If you are successful, your students can easily develop a mental picture of what you are teaching them.

The establishment of an internalized impression of the movement is important for several reasons. First, it provides the basis for the students' actions; their actions are guided by the image they hold in their mind. Second, it produces a mental model of the physical action required by indicating the composition of the movement. This gives direct feedback for the practitioner after every trial. And it prevents unnecessary injuries that might occur due to the ignorance of how to perform the movement correctly.

Once the students have established a mental image of the technique, the next step is consistent and intensive practice. Diligent practice increases speed, accuracy and the ability to adapt the technique to meet the demands of a real situation. Also, through practice, the mental demands in executing a skill decrease in direct relation to the amount of time and effort invested. When a student nears mastery level of a particular technique, he can perform with very little sensory guidance.

*Practice is a
daily necessity
for martial arts
students of all
ability levels.*

The Progression of Physical Practice

1. Initial goal setting
2. Formation of mental image
3. Rudimentary physical model of movement
4. Physical practice
5. Increase in speed and accuracy
6. Application
7. Practice in applications
8. Development of automatic movement
9. Internalization
10. Mastery

Practice does not, however, always result in mastery. The mastery of a skill will only be acquired if practice is approached with the firm intention of improving the designated skill. Encourage your students to practice with the seriousness needed to improve. Never allow them to practice mechanically with minimal attention to their performance. When you see that they are serious about practicing, you can increase the intensity of their practice. The more they practice, the higher level of skill they will attain.

Practicing with the firm intention of improving is made possible through self-discipline. Discipline is a fundamental goal of martial arts and practice is a means to achieve that goal. Only a disciplined practice schedule can lead to mastery of an art. Mere mechanical practice never generates proficiency, but only leaves students with bad habits and boredom that generally increase the dropout rate of a school.

Mental Practice

Perfect practice is possible only when your training has a balance of mental and physical practice. With physical practice alone, you will never gain a high level of proficiency in the martial arts. In fact, you may actually get tired of what you are doing long before you ever reach your desired level of performance. In addition to physical practice, you need mental practice, which is the non-physical rehearsal of a movement. To mentally practice a movement, think about the movement in great detail and visualize yourself performing it perfectly.

Imagine yourself performing a flying side kick. As you visualize yourself jumping, you may feel your leg muscles twitch and your heart rate speed up. The momentary rush of excitement you feel is caused by the electrical impulses occurring in your brain. If you create a vivid image in your mind, your brain will activate the same neural impulses in your body as it does when you physically execute the movement. This is an effective way of preparing your body for an accurate, confident performance.

Mental practice is the most effective way to teach new skills. If you demonstrate the purpose of the movement and how to perform it correctly, the student will be able to form an accurate mental picture of what he should do. Once the student has learned a rudimentary version of the skill, mental practice can be used to enhance his performance. By comparing his execution of a movement with his mental image of the movement, he can refine his skills and remove bad habits. As the student begins practicing complex, advanced movements, he can use mental practice to reduce errors, increase concentration and improve strategy.

There are two methods of mental practice. The first is **Action Visualization**, which is used to learn a new skill such as a front kick. Begin by focusing on the correct way to execute the front kick. Visualize yourself executing the kick with perfect balance, accuracy and coordination. Start slowly and build speed and power gradually. By consistently using Action Visualization, you can dramatically improve your technical performance and concentration.

The second method is called **Reaction Visualization**. This is used to improve interactive skills like sparring and self-defense by imagining how to react to a specific situation in the ring or in the street. Visualize your opponent delivering a thrust kick or a lunge punch. Think about how you should react. See yourself responding with a combination of counter attacks with strong determination and quick reflexes. You can do this type of strategy rehearsal almost anywhere in about five minutes. Pre-experiencing many possible situations increases your confidence and insight into training.

You can lead you students in metal practice before or after class or at set intervals during practice. Use it frequently and encourage students to incorporate it into their personal practice sessions. Through mental practice your students will show more motivation and confidence in their physical performance.

Taking time out for mental practice through meditation or visualization is helpful to motivate a more confident physical performance.

Discipline

Martial arts without discipline is an empty pursuit. Martial arts start from discipline and become discipline. Without discipline, learning cannot occur. If it does, it can be dangerous. Martial arts knowledge is as much a deadly weapon as a gun or a knife. According to how and when you use it, it can be destructive or constructive.

Generally there are two kinds of discipline: preventive and remedial (corrective) discipline. **Preventive discipline** is a positive process of learning guided by the pursuit of a common and specific goal. In this environment everyone is expected to voluntarily work together toward the same goal. Preventive discipline is the ultimate goal of every teacher. **Remedial discipline** is a process of recognizing and correcting undesirable behavior. This serves to return the group to a positive course of action so preventive discipline can again prevail.

In a martial arts school, discipline must begin from the day the student signs up for class. Therefore the following criteria must be clearly presented to and understood by the beginner:

1. What the student can expect to learn (initial goal setting)
2. The basic content and format of the class
3. The rules he is expected to follow
4. The importance of regular attendance and practice

All school rules must be specific and well defined. Every new student should have access to a written list of the school rules and procedures. The rules should be consistent and applied to everyone equally. The consequences of breaking or ignoring the rules must be clearly identified and enforced. Additionally, the following criteria must be understood by the instructor:

1. The specific needs of the student
2. The physical and mental limitations of the student

The more accurate information you have about a student the easier it is to place him into the correct class level and to provide appropriate goals and instruction.

The instructor should always know what level the student is at, what skills he needs to improve or perfect, and how he feels about his present progress. Gaining ongoing information about students and continuously developing plans in terms of your students are important factors in school management. Effective class discipline is a result of careful planning and proper implementation. By learning to predict student behavior, you can successfully implement preventive discipline.

Another method of preventive discipline is setting and upholding the curriculum standards of your class. Letting students pass through a particular course or belt level without learning the required skills will not result in a positive learning experience. They must understand that following The Way (Do) and mastering the necessary skills with endurance is the best way to progress.

Teach a tempered concept of "No pain, no gain" from the beginning and throughout the learning process. This attitude, balanced with constructive, enjoyable activities creates a challenging learning environment. In this environment, students are willing to try new things and can discover their optimal level of performance.

Finally, the most important point for an instructor to consider in terms of discipline is his or her own conduct. An instructor's behavior and performance pattern cannot be separated from the performance pattern of his class. The instructor is the initiator of disciplinary motivation for his students. Student behavior is a direct result of the instructor's interaction with the class, the student performance requirements for each level, and the frequency of goal attainment. If students sense that their instructor has the knowledge and skills he is requiring from them, they will see him as a model and be eager to imitate his performance.

Student discipline is directly related to instructor conduct.

Respect

Martial arts training begins with learning how to respect the tradition of the art and the school. One of the first actions of respect that a student learns is how and when to bow. A beginner student probably feels uncomfortable when he bows to the flags and to his seniors. Though he does not want to bow, he knows that it is proper, so he does it. Gradually, the act of bowing becomes natural and without bowing he feels that something is missing. Eventually as he becomes a higher belt in the school, he starts to find something deeper within the action of bowing.

When performing a bow, the serious student exchanges silent communications with his classmates or instructors. When bowing to the flags, he feels something different from the experience of learning kicking and punching and obeying the rules. He learns one of the most critical things in martial arts training - silent communication. He realizes the invisible relationships he has with the world around him that transcend the time limits of the past, present and future. He feels his connection to the traditions and history of the art. No one can teach this or explain it. You have to experience it directly.

Respect comes from this realization of our true relationship with others and with ourselves. Respect is a genuine acknowledgment of the important value of others and of ourselves. It is both mutual and contagious. When you don't respect your students there will be no respect in return, and you shouldn't expect it.

To promote respect in your school, recognize the importance of every individual regardless of their physical condition, status, or any other preconceptions you might have. If a student resists your efforts and is openly disrespectful, try to approach him with respect as a fellow human being. If this doesn't work, be patient. To share true friendship takes time. Once you succeed in reaching the student, you can begin to show him how to have respect. Respect can never be taught. It must be shown and caught.

Teaching students to follow the school rules and tradition is the first step toward teaching them to respect others. For example, one of the rules at my school is that all students must keep their toenails and fingernails trimmed.

This rule promotes respect for others by ensuring that your training partner does not receive an unnecessary injury. It would be disrespectful to kick your partner and give him a severe laceration because you were too lazy to cut your toenails. Another rule states that all students must keep their uniforms clean. This rule promotes self-respect by encouraging the student to pay attention to and take pride in his personal appearance.

Although these rules do not directly teach respect, they set up guidelines for the students to follow in terms of their behavior toward others. Of course you cannot expect a beginner to immediately gain a sense of respect because of these rules. However, the tradition of the martial arts deserves respect and acknowledgment.

Respect for the tradition of the art is an excellent starting point to open the door to trusting others. Every student has in common the fact that he is learning martial arts. As time goes by, this common bond will establish a spirit of togetherness. During this critical period of bonding, you can direct students toward mutual respect through group activities or individual counseling.

Another factor that encourages the growth of self-respect within a student is the step-by-step process of rank promotion. With every promotion, the student's pride and confidence increases, as does his self-respect. Building respect is a long term process. An instructor and students should realize this to be successful in building respect. Both must work together toward one goal. There is no one-sided teaching. It must be mutual.

Therefore, to instill respect, you must be a person who respects the tradition of the art you teach, respects other people and most of all, respects yourself. Your students will naturally sense if you are a person who deserves respect. When your students respect you, you can shape their attitude toward the art and toward their lives. When every martial arts student respects their family, friends, and teachers, our community holds great promise for the future.

Respect both in and outside of class the classroom is an essential attribute of martial arts education.

Curriculum

The map is not the territory.

- Alfred Korzbybski

Chapter 4
Curriculum Development

Every individual has different reasons and motives for learning martial arts. Some people want to become good competitors, while others want to increase their confidence and gain inner peace. An instructor must be able to teach every student the full concept of the art without ignoring their individual needs. You need a complete vision of your teaching plan. What you teach must be sufficiently consistent and knowledgeable to lead your students toward their goals. Every step in your teaching should lead to the physical progress and mental growth of your students.

In a martial arts school, the curriculum is vast and varied. Students learn combat skills through sparring and self-defense, improve internal awareness and discipline through form practice and seek inner peace through meditation. In addition to these topics, there are many subjects that vary from school to school. In this chapter are the most fundamentally important subjects for a martial arts curriculum. According to the style of martial arts that you are teaching, you can implement these subjects in the way that fits best for your situation.

It is vitally important to plan what to teach so individual classes are balanced. For example, if you plan to teach warming-up exercises, sparring, forms and weapons skills in a sixty minute class, the time proportion for each segment must be decided in advance. Many instructors have had the experience of starting with warming-up exercises, then reviewing basic skills, only to find that 45 minutes have already passed. Of course, they know that 15 minutes is not enough time to teach both forms and sparring. On the other hand delegating exactly 15 minutes for each subject without regard for the content of the lesson makes class boring and monotonous. Poor planning leaves students feeling tired and unbalanced.

Beyond the number of subjects and content you plan to teach, consider such mitigating factors as extremely hot or cold weather, the attitude and condition of your students, the possibility of an upcoming tournament or promotion, etc. These situations change the immediate needs of your students and you must adapt your teaching accordingly.

This chapter covers a broad spectrum of individual topics. Based on these subjects, you can develop more ideas through experience and experimentation.

Conditioning

Martial arts training requires the use of almost every muscle in the body. Therefore, it is very important to do a complete regimen of conditioning exercises before beginning difficult class activities. Conditioning exercises perform several important functions.

♦ By elevating the metabolism in the body, the various physiological systems are prepared for more rigorous physical activity.

♦ The circulation in the body increases and the nervous system becomes more sensitive, allowing for sharper reflexes.

♦ The flexibility of the muscles and the range of motion of the joints increases through the use of a variety of stretching exercises.

♦ Primary muscle groups increase in strength, reducing the possibility of injury and allowing the student to progress naturally to more difficult movements.

For optimal conditioning, two to three intensive workouts per week are recommended. Days of intensive training should be alternated with days of light training or rest. At least 10-15 minutes of warming-up is strongly recommended before engaging in sudden change of direction movements or physical contact activities. This is especially true for spinning kicks and full power techniques.

There are five categories of conditioning exercises:

1) Warm-up exercises
2) Stretching
3) Balance Exercises
4) Strength Exercises
5) Endurance Exercises.

On the following pages are sample exercises from each of the four groups. A detailed explanation for each can be found in the book *Ultimate Fitness through Martial Arts* (Turtle Press, 1993). Using a regular program of these or similar exercises will greatly enhance your students' general physical condition.

1. Warm-up Exercises

Begin every workout with warm-up exercises. They are the best way to raise the body temperature and loosen the joints and muscles. They also increase the circulation in the body to lubricate joints and muscles. There are two methods of warm-up exercises: extremities to trunk or trunk to extremities. When you work extremities to trunk, begin with the wrists, ankles and neck and work inward to the large joints and muscle groups of the trunk. Conversely when working trunk to extremities , begin with the hips and chest and work outward to the wrists, ankles and neck.

a. jumping jacks
b. neck rotation
c. shoulder rotation
d. hip rotation
e. knee rotation
f. trunk twisting (side to side)
g. upper body rotation
h. standing toe touch (alternate side to side)
i. jumping spin
j. knee touch
k. bounding
l. sprinting
m. side scoop
n. star jumps
o. bicycling

2. Stretching Exercises

Stretching exercises increase the range of motion of the body by increasing flexibility and elasticity in the muscles. Begin with a light stretch and proceed to a full stretch when the muscles are fully warmed-up. When planning stretching exercises, group them according to standing, seated and prone exercises to avoid unnecessary movement. Teach students to stretch to an uncomfortable but not painful point. Discomfort indicates progress but pain indicates a breakdown in muscle tissue and results in poor muscle quality. Also avoid ballistic stretching and overstretching caused by putting too much weight on the extended muscle.

a. finger press
b. neck muscle stretching
c. chest expansion
d. trunk stretch - side
e. trunk stretch - front/back
f. palm to floor touch (standing)
g. knee press
h. hurdler's stretch
i. split to each side and center
j. stretching with partner
k. front kick stretch

l. side kick stretch
m. back kick stretch
n. leg swing
o. bridge
p. shoulder standing
q. arm raises and circles
r. half windmills
s. seated trunk twist
t. back roll
u. butterfly stretch
v. double quad stretch

3. Balance Exercises

Balance exercises improve spatial awareness and posture as well as stability. All three attributes are important for strong offensive and defensive capabilities in sparring and self-defense. Practice balance exercises slowly and with attention to the goal of the movement. For jumping exercises, focus maintaining good posture in the air and landing with balance and control.

a. jumping rope (alternate speed/style)
b. hopping on one leg
c. quickly switching legs (simultaneously)
d. 360 degree jump and spin
e. jump and touch knees to chest
f. jump and touch toes with legs extended
g. jump and touch toes behind body
h. jump over a rope or other moving object
i. head stand
j. hand stand
k. walking on hands
l. pushing kicks
m. single leg stretch
n. single leg squat
o. windmill
p. partner bridge

4. Strength Exercises

Strength exercises focus on the development of specific muscles to improve skills. Increases in strength training should be gradual and progressive. Consistent training is the key to improvement.

a. push-ups
b. sit-ups
c. right and left side sit-ups
d. back sit-ups
e. leg lifting
f. hopping in squatting position
g. one leg squats
h. chin-ups
i. hand stand push-ups
j. V-ups
k. lunges
l. standing jump
m. calf raises

standing jump

5. ENDURANCE EXERCISES

Endurance exercises raise the respiration and heart rate and increase lung capacity. They should mobilize muscles to their tiring point repetitively to increase the muscles' capacity for work. There are two types of endurance training: aerobic and anaerobic. Aerobic exercise literally means "with oxygen". It is exercise that relies on the body's continuous intake of oxygen to supply energy to the muscles. An example of aerobic endurance training is distance running. Anaerobic exercises are those that require more oxygen than the body is able to take in through breathing. They rely on energy stored in the body. An example of anaerobic endurance training is interval training.

You can determine the type of exercise you are doing by your breathing. If you can carry on a normal conversation during endurance exercise, you are doing aerobic exercise. If your breathing is labored and continues to be long after you finish exercising, you are doing anaerobic exercise. When teaching children, keep in mind that they have very limited anaerobic capacity until they begin to mature physically at the onset of puberty.

    a. interval running
    b. uphill/stair running
    c. shadow sparring
    d. distance running
    e. isometric exercises
    f. heavy bag workout
    g. stair running
    h. sparring

When the body is well conditioned with a proper warm-up, the coordination of mind and body will increase and the combined physical and mental response to any situation will be quickened.

Basic Movements

It is impossible to describe all the fundamental movements of every martial art in this book, because every martial art has its own unique system of basic skills. However, we will cover general ideas that you can use as a guide in teaching.

In teaching basic movements to beginners, start with an explanation of how the parts of the human body are used in your style of martial art. Explain both the body parts that can be used offensively and those that can be used defensively.   Then begin to teach the student specifically how to use each part of the body correctly, such as middle punch, high block, front kick, etc.

The basic movements of most styles include hand techniques, foot techniques, and hand-foot combinations. Footwork and body shifting can be combined with these fundamentals for realistic applications. There are four types of primary body shifting methods: forward, backward, to the right and to the left. At the advanced level, fundamental directional movements can be combined with lunging, jumping, hopping, skipping, turning and angular movements.

In addition to agile footwork, teach your students to always maintain correct stances and good posture. Correct stances and posture enables them to execute with speed and prevents them from developing idiosyncratic habits that telegraph their intentions before an attack.

To improve the accuracy of attacking techniques, teach the vital points of the human body. When students know where the exact target areas are on the body, they can correctly apply every attack. For example, instead of doing a high section roundhouse kick, middle section front kick and low section side kick, the well trained student does a roundhouse kick to the temple, a front kick to the solar plexus and a side kick to the knee joint. **Target visualization** allows your students to practice in a focused manner with the intention of improving.

Based on personal progress, you can teach combinations of these skills. For example, stepping forward back foot side kick to the ribs or stepping backward left hand high block and right hand middle punch to the solar plexus. In using a progressive approach to teaching fundamentals, your students will measure their progress in steady, concrete steps. Allow advanced students to create their own complex combinations to encourage them to practice fundamentals regularly. They will find that the variations on even the most basic techniques are limitless.

Basics are the most important part of your curriculum. Teaching slowly and correctly is better than pouring all of your knowledge into an unsuspecting white belt. Give your students the chance to understand every step correctly. If you give too much explanation, they will become overwhelmed. Explain key points and allow them to explore and discover the movement. Keep your teaching simple and to the point.

Forms

In the martial arts, the performance of forms is the most structured expression of the art. For every form there is an ideal way of performing. It is this ideal that the forms practitioner seeks to reach through consistent practice. First, he practices to perfect the pattern of the movements. Next he works to implement the intrinsic attributes of the form including speed, power and timing. Finally, he strives to attain total mental and physical unity through the realization of an ideal performance. It is through this process of mastery that the beauty of the martial arts is truly understood.

Every traditional system has its own set of forms (poomse, kata, hyung) that increase in difficulty as the student progresses. In the early days of martial art, forms were the only method of passing on the secrets of the art from master to student. Thus, each form is a series of offensive and defensive movements arranged in a meaningful order for combat against imaginary opponents. The blocks, strikes, kicks and stances of each form are well suited to the student's current level and increase in difficulty with each succeeding form.

Form practice is very important because without understanding the art of forms, it is almost impossible to understand the total concept of a martial art. Through the practice of forms, students develop coordination, focus, breath control, balance, strength, flexibility, discipline, endurance and peace of mind.

Every form in every style of martial arts has its own meaning and character. To master the form, understanding its character is as necessary as remembering the sequence of the movements. When teaching forms, start by explaining the meaning of each movement and demonstrating how to perform it step-by-step. Once the individual movements have been learned correctly, the next step is to practice the entire form until the student can complete it without thought or external distraction. At this point he can begin to understand the intrinsic unity and meaning of the form.

Tips for Teaching a New Form

1. The ready stance should be calm and relaxed yet full of potential energy.

2. Clearly explain the sequence and pattern of movements.

3. Teach every movement slowly and precisely. Be sure the students are moving in the correct direction and are placing their hands and feet in the proper position.

4. Teach correct posture and eye direction for each movement.

5. The execution of movements should be smooth, dynamic, and decisive. The mind and body should be relaxed between movements.

6. Emphasize controlled breathing and a strong explosive yell (kiai/kihap) where required.

7. Demonstrate how to combine the different types of power required for forms. Slow, fluid movements and strong explosive movements should flow smoothly into each other.

8. Teach the meaning of each form and emphasize practicing it as if in a real combat situation.

9. Allow students to practice the form facing in different directions.

10. Teach the next form only after the student refines the preceding forms.

As your students progress to higher forms, they will develop a strong, confident martial spirit. Their character will become well-rounded and they will realize that their art is useful for more than defeating an opponent.

Sparring

In martial arts training, there are many styles of sparring: non-contact, light contact, controlled contact and full contact. Which style you teach depends on your training background and the needs of your students. Whatever style your students will ultimately practice, start with prearranged sparring and progress to non-contact sparring. From the intermediate stage, varying degrees of contact can be introduced based on student interest.

There are two ways of teaching sparring: prearranged sparring and free sparring. Prearranged sparring must be taught before students are allowed to engage in free sparring. By practicing predetermined attacks and counterattacks, students learn the importance of using precise, controlled techniques in sparring practice.

In prearranged sparring, two students face each other in fighting stance. The student acting as the attacker executes a predetermined kick or strike (or combination of both). The defender responds with a predetermined block and counter. Initially, in prearranged sparring, all the movements must be carefully choreographed according to the students' skill level. In time, you can designate the attack and allow the defender to block and counter freely. This will allow the beginning student to develop the attributes of timing, judgment, reflexes and distance in a controlled environment.

For the beginner who is afraid of the aggressive nature of sparring, prearranged sparring is a safe method of introducing the concepts and strategies of sparring. Conversely, for the overzealous student, prearranged sparring will teach control.

By the time students reach the intermediate level, they will be ready for free sparring. Free sparring can be divided into two areas of strategy: offensive (initiative attack style) and defensive (counterattack style). At first it is best to teach initiative attacking because action is simpler and quicker than reaction. When initiative attacking skills become quicker and stronger, the gradual introduction of countering methods provides the other half of sparring.

In the advanced stage, when students have internalized initiative attacks, begin teaching more complex counterattacking skills and strategies. These techniques require good reflexes, but they are more effective than initiative attacks. One of the most difficult types of counterattacking skills is trapping. Trapping is accomplished by luring the opponent into a desired action by a combination of fakes and/or attacks. The fakes, through sudden upper body movement or footwork, are used to break the opponent's defense and set-up a scoring attack.

When teaching prearranged or free sparring consider the following:

1. Always use safety equipment including hand and foot gear, chest protectors, head gear, mouthpiece and groin guard.

2. Teach clearly and be certain that students understand what they should do. (See Chapter 5 for more on methods)

3. Each student should practice his strong and weak sides and skills equally.

4. Everyone should practice with full concentration. Do not allow mechanical performance.

5. Develop speed gradually. The irony in speed training is that to become fast you must begin practicing slowly.

6. Teach from simple techniques toward more complex ones.

7. Practice techniques with footwork so that students can learn to use skills in dynamic situations.

Most importantly, in sparring, as in all aspects of training, practice should be regular and consistent. Through regular sparring, students will improve their endurance and discover the mental and physical cycles of their body. In competition or in self-defense, this knowledge is vital for survival and victory over the opponent.

Sparring practice can take many forms including prearranged, non-contact practice (left) and full contact competition (below).

Self-Defense

We are living in a highly civilized environment compared to any other period in history. We have many laws to protect ourselves and preserve the order of society. Unfortunately, crime rates are soaring higher every day. Not a single day passes without violence committed against innocent people. Without a perfect solution to crime, everyone needs a means of defense to protect himself and his loved ones. As a member of society, every person has a right to protection from an unlawful attack.

For this purpose, many people turn to martial arts. As a martial arts instructor, you are responsible for giving these people the ability to keep themselves safe and to live without fear. You can do this by teaching them self-defense skills and how and when to use them.

There are many techniques that can be applied in every situation. Analyze the needs of each student and determine the techniques that are best for his or her size, strength, age and ability. For beginners, teach simple, effective movements that are easy to remember and can apply to a variety of situations.

Beginners are looking for realism. They will go home and try to use these techniques on their friends and relatives to see if they really work. Teach them realistic skills like striking vital areas (eyes, throat, groin, nose, shins, knees) and remind them of the serious damage these attacks can do when executed correctly.

In the intermediate and advanced stages, begin teaching joint locks and throws. Teach these skills slowly and progressively and prepare students fully. Before you teach throwing, teach the correct method of falling to prevent back and neck injuries. Also, caution students to stop applying pressure to a joint as soon as their partner gives the signal to stop. With careful supervision, your students can enjoy learning complex, useful techniques for self-defense.

Most importantly, in teaching self-defense, emphasize that none of the skills learned in class should be used in any situation without a valid reason. Inform students of the laws in your state regarding the use of force in a self-defense situation.

Principles for Self-Defense:

1. Recognize potentially dangerous situations.

2. Avoid dangerous situations. This is the best method of self-defense.

3. Escape, if you can, using any method.

4. If your attacker wants material possessions give them to him. Do not risk your life for money or possessions.

5. Defend yourself as a last resort. Commit yourself totally, decisively, powerfully, and quickly.

Self-Defense Psychology:

1. Calm down and relax. You are still alive.

2. Try to communicate with your assailant as a person.

3. Do not aggravate the assailant.

4. Try to make the assailant relaxed and off guard and attack when he least expects it.

5. Apply all means possible, without hesitation, to save your life.

Meditation

Anxiety is a natural arousal of the human body caused by external or internal stimuli. When anxiety is eliminated or reduced, the mind becomes spontaneous and capable. In Eastern culture, people have often practiced a form of contemplation, called Zazen or Joasun, to reduce anxiety and attain enlightenment. In the West, this practice is commonly known as meditation. Meditation is a state of deep relaxation. It is also a state of alertness. Although this sounds contradictory to the novice, it is a unified idea. In meditation, the mind is calm and at peace with its surroundings.

Meditation is an important part of martial arts class. It may be practiced before and after class. Mentally, it gives students a heightened sense of concentration and it deepens their sense of self. Physically, it improves performance because speed and accuracy are increased when the body is relaxed.

It is also helpful for children. Quiet time helps them calm down before class or recover after a tiring activity. Without mentioning meditation, just let them sit and close their eyes. The rest will come naturally. If they get distracted, gently remind them to return to the activity. In time you may be pleasantly surprised to find them using meditation on their own initiative.

For the adult student, meditation takes on a more serious meaning. Though you cannot exactly teach students to meditate correctly, you can guide them. Traditionally meditation is done in a seated position, but this is up to the individual. Whatever position you choose, relax your body. If you choose to open your eyes, focus on a point in front of you but not on a specific object.

Concentrate on your breathing. Be aware of the rhythm of inhaling and exhaling. Breathe as you normally do with your mouth naturally closed. Empty your mind of all conscious thoughts. If an unwanted thought enters your mind, let it come and go naturally. Don't fight it. Meditation should flow freely.

At first, it is very difficult to maintain concentration and hold the mind. Simply forget about trying. Attempting to achieve something through meditation only leads to frustration. Success comes when you least expect it. It can only be found through diligent practice. In meditation, the mind must not be hurried. It must be firm and composed. This is the state of mind that upholds the martial artist's spirit.

Through properly guided meditation, students build inner confidence and composure. They feel at ease with themselves. The feel free from stress because they have a means to control their emotions. They can then face life's challenges with freedom and composure.

Breath Control

Breathing is the only method that humans have for taking in oxygen. Without it, our life cannot continue. The entire balance of our body is controlled by our breathing. In martial arts, breathing has a special significance. By taking in the right amount of air, you can make your body momentarily hard and immune to attack by the opponent. By exhaling sharply and suddenly, a total integration of energy occurs and your muscles tighten and work as one unit.

This exhalation is often accompanied by a sound known as kiai or kihap. Although kihap sounds like shouting, its origin is different. Kihap occurs when the energy of the body causes the muscles to tighten and the exhaling air is forced through a small opening. The result is a loud sound originating in the lower abdomen. The phenomena of kihap can be compared to boiling water. If the water boils in an open pot it makes only a quiet rumbling sound. However if you boil water in a teapot with only a small hole in the top, the result is a loud whistle as the air is released from the pot.

Kihap enables you to concentrate fully your mind and body for maximum power. Kihap also can help relieve inner fear and allow you to weaken your opponent psychologically.

Most importantly, by controlling your breathing, you control the way your body uses its precious energy supply. The body's natural reaction to an oxygen deficit is to take fast, shallow breaths. This is not the most efficient way to supply oxygen to your muscles. By breathing slowly and deeply when you are tired, you take in more oxygen over a longer period. By breathing deeply, you create a richer supply of oxygen in the blood and consequently your muscles recover quicker and work harder.

Also, in combat or competition it is recommended to conceal your breathing patterns. A skilled opponent can take advantage of your lack of concealment by attacking you when you are inhaling, thereby making a counterattack momentarily impossible.

The Theory of Power

The ideal fighter is a person who can consistently and accurately hit a target with maximum power and speed while maintaining full control, mentally and physically. While few people ever reach this ideal, an instructor's job is to guide students toward this model. The primary function of any teaching is to find the potential of every student and develop it to the highest possible level. This level varies according to the individual, but there is a way to maximize everyone's ability.

You can assist your students in achieving optimum performance levels by improving their muscle strength, muscle endurance, flexibility, speed, coordination, accuracy and concentration. These elements make up the Theory of Power. By showing students how these elements interact in their daily training, you will enable them to realize their full potential.

Elements of Power

1. Strength

2. Speed

3. Flexibility

4. Focus

5. Coordination

6. Accuracy

7. Integration of mental and physical skills

Power is force exerted over time. In scientific terms, power is expressed as force times velocity. Physiologically, force is dependent on muscle strength and velocity is dependent on speed. If you want to apply power over an extended period, endurance also becomes important.

Muscular strength is the ability to effectively apply force against resistance. Stronger muscles give you greater movement potential and naturally improve your performance. The easiest and most inexpensive way to improve strength is to adopt a regimen of simple muscle building exercises including push-ups, sit-ups, squats, knee to chest jumping, and interval running (sprints).

Weight training is also a good way to build strength in the major muscle groups. Weight training for martial arts should emphasize light weights and high repetitions to maintain flexibility and to build endurance. Speed and flexibility are as important as strength and one should not be developed at the expense of the other.

In strength training, work the muscles specific to the art itself, especially the large muscle groups in the legs and trunk. Allow at least 48 hours between workouts for each muscle group. If you work your lower body Monday, work your upper body Tuesday. This will allow the muscle cells to heal themselves. It is the healing process that causes the muscles to increase in size, so this process should not be interrupted. Pace yourself well and increase gradually for the best results.

As your muscle strength improves, your speed will follow naturally. There are also ways to increase speed independently of strength. Speed originates in the fast-twitch muscle fibers. The best exercises to strengthen the fast-twitch fibers are explosive exercises like wind sprints. When doing speed training concentrate on creating explosive initial movements and letting the rest of the action flow naturally. Focus on a lightning start and just let the rest of your steps follow until the original energy has dissipated. Then start over.

As a component of speed you should work on improving your reflexes. Reflexes can be thought of as mental speed and must be trained just as you train for physical speed. The best way to sharpen your reflexes is to expose yourself repeatedly to situations in which you must choose and execute one of several possible responses. Feedback should be immediate. For example, have your training partner hold two hand targets behind his back. He randomly thrusts one of them toward you and you strike it with an appropriate kick or strike. You will have immediate feedback in hitting or missing the target.

Strength and speed are the fundamentals of power, but they are influenced greatly by a presence or absence of flexibility, coordination and balance. Flexibility is important because it allows you to use you body's full range of motion. Without flexibility, your performance is limited before you begin. Becoming more flexible is a slow process, but through consistent use of stretching and joint conditioning exercises you should begin to see measurable improvement in as little as 3 months. Using breathing exercises during stretching and drinking plenty of water daily will enhance the response of your muscles by keeping them supplied with an adequate amount of oxygen.

As every beginner martial artist experiences, without coordination and balance, it is difficult to execute techniques correctly. Both elements are essential to performing the rapid combinations required for sparring, forms and self-defense. The best way to improve coordination is to practice new movements slowly and to break them into smaller parts if necessary. As the movement feels natural, increase speed, complexity and power. This improves coordination and increase confidence in the movement.

As you study the Theory of Power it becomes obvious that it is made up of many interdependent parts. A good balance of these elements is important. Yet, no matter how much power you can generate, it will amount to nothing if you don't have a good sense of timing and accuracy. You can throw the most powerful blow in the world at your opponent but if you don't hit him, you have only succeeded in wasting energy.

Good timing comes from a relaxed mind. When you are relaxed, you are naturally in tune with the rhythm of your body. This is critical in knowing when to attack and when to wait. Accuracy can be acquired by learning every movement correctly from the beginning. Always practice with full concentration and focus on the execution of every technique. The best technique is when you can strike the target while it is motion.

Up to this point I have only discussed the physical aspects of the Theory of Power. Physical ability is only part of creating power. The real power in martial arts comes from the mind. The superior power that martial artists strive in earnest to possess is rooted in mental power. The body is only the tool with which to deliver the power of the mind. Once you have honed the tool to perfection, the potential for its use is limitless.

Running on sand is a time honored way of developing leg strength.

Methodology

One may explain water
but the mouth will not
become wet.

- Takuan

Chapter 5
Teaching Methodology

Historically, teaching has been called both an art and a science. The artistic viewpoint contends that since teaching is humans giving knowledge to humans, it must place flexibility, moral values and emotional consideration as the first priorities. On the contrary, the scientific viewpoint holds that teaching is a disciplined process that must follow a system of rules and doctrines to be successful.

Most teachers find that a balanced combination of art and science produces the best results in the classroom. A structured curriculum and disciplinary method tempered by flexibility and sensitivity to the needs of the students creates a positive learning environment. In your teaching, find the balance that best suits your personality and the atmosphere of your school.

Avoid the extremes in teaching. An overly structured and disciplined atmosphere discourages innovation and natural skill development. Conversely, a classroom without structure makes students insecure and unfocused. If your classes start moving toward one extreme, gently guide them back to the desired equilibrium.

This chapter is designed as a guide to assist you in structuring your curriculum (scientific viewpoint) and implementing it in your daily teaching (artistic viewpoint).

Curriculum Structure

Skillful teaching requires a structured curriculum that applies to students at each skill level. Martial art curriculum is based on the following progression of learning:

1. Learning how to condition the body
2. Learning how to defend oneself
3. Learning about the art
4. Developing inner strength and spirit
5. Integrating the mind and body

I have provided a sample curriculum structure as a guide. Not every element will fit into your teaching, however, you will probably find a related concept in your art. For example, under the Intermediate - Supplementary Training Methods, heavy bag kicking is indicated because the intermediate stage is the time for developing powerful techniques. If you have a different way of developing power in your art, the intermediate stage is the time to use it. Analyze each stage for intent rather than content. Find the best way to teach your art based on the structure below.

In addition to the objectives and teaching methods for each stage, the curriculum structure should include appropriate skills for each level (i.e. basic movements, combinations, self-defense skills, prearranged sparring sets, etc.). Depending on the specificity of your teaching, arrange skills by belt level or general skill level. Update your curriculum structure regularly as you develop new teaching and training skills to keep your teaching fresh and alive.

Beginner Stage (0 to 6 months)

Objective	Introduce the new student to fundamental movements and school rules
Prerequisite	Meet instructor's criteria for acceptance as a student
Teaching techniques	1. Establish primary and intermediate goals 2. Give the student a mental picture of how to perform each new skill correctly to allow for internal feedback 3. Teach through simple verbal explanations and demonstrations. 4. Provide background information on language, history and traditions.
Supplementary training:	1. Use wall mounted stretching bar for flexibility and basic coordination 2. Weight training for general fitness
Possible reasons for dropouts	1. Frustration due to physical shortcomings 2. Frustration because class is moving too fast/slow 3. Class does not meet student's expectations 4. Difficulty adjusting to class schedule 5. Fatigue or pain
Solutions	1. Simplify teaching methods 2. Be flexible in pacing the class 3. Teach realistic skills 4. Be sensitive to individual needs and differences 5. Combine aerobic and anaerobic training 6. Provide positive feedback

Intermediate Stage (7 months to 2 years)

Objective	Integration of individual movements
Prerequisites	1. Successful completion of beginner course 2. Strong basic skills
Teaching techniques	1. Emphasize improving the transitions between movements through combination drills 2. Practice timing and spatial awareness in controlled partner drills 3. Remove extraneous movements and streamline basic skills 4. Increase power and speed in training
Supplementary training	1. Heavy bag workout 2. Target kicking and striking (hand target and mitts) 3. Zigzag running 4. Jumping rope
Possible reasons for dropouts	1. Overtraining injuries 2. Lack of goals or motivation 3. Loss of initial excitement of beginner stage 4. Plateau in physical improvement
Solutions:	1. Perfect basics 2. Provide specific goals 3. Provide positive feedback 4. Teach new skills progressively 5. Supplement training with strength building exercise

Advanced Stage (2 to 3 years)	
Objective	Organization, speed and accuracy of skills
Prerequisites	1. Successful completion of Intermediate course 2. Smooth, fluid execution of skills
Teaching techniques	1. Improve timing through reflex drills 2. Encourage automatic execution of skills 3. Provide opportunities for internal motivation to develop through self-guided practice
Supplementary training	1. In-depth training for speed, reflexes 2. Muscle-specific strengthening exercises
Possible reasons for dropouts	1. Student learned enough to meet original goal 2. Boredom with lack of new skills 3. Frustration in learning advanced skills due to a lack of sound fundamentals
Solutions	1. Provide higher goals 2. Teach how to create complex skills by combining simple skills 3. Emphasize perfection of fundamentals 4. Upgrade the intensity of strength training so the student is able to cope with the increased physical demands of training 5. Teach the philosophical component of training

Black Belt Stage (3 years +)

Objective	To learn the complex concepts and master the intrinsic essence of the art
Prerequisites	1. Successful completion of Advanced Course 2. Commitment to training and proper attitude
Teaching techniques	1. Teach complex skills and strategies 2. Give ample time for self-discovery 3. Provide information on the history, traditions and philosophy of the art 4. Teach kinetic theory and physics 5. Encourage students to receive training in first aid and CPR
Supplementary training	1. Video analysis of performance 2. Develop understanding of the intricacies of the art through assistant teaching
Possible reasons for dropouts	1. False sense of mastery 2. Early ambition to open a martial arts school 3. False expectation of being a black belt 4. Unable to meet black belt requirements
Solutions	1. Emphasize the new beginning of black belt training 2. Provide teaching opportunities 3. Insist on perfection of basic skills 4. Instill a sense of responsibility 5. Provide leadership skill training

Creating Lesson Plans

With this overview of curriculum structure in mind, we can examine how to create a lesson plan. Daily planning is essential in effectively implementing your ideas. To create a lesson plan, first **consider your objectives**. List your objectives for the class in a simple format. Based on those objectives, plan the subjects to include in the class.

Highlight new skills and prepare a brief introduction for each. Also designate ample practice following the introduction of new skills. Next, consider the **rhythm of the class**. Alternate periods of activity with periods of rest for best results. There are two complementary methods of setting the rhythm: high intensity with frequent rest periods or low intensity with few rest periods. High intensity training is best for reviewing skills and endurance training. Low intensity training is recommended for new skills because tired muscles create poor imitations of new skills and mental fatigue impedes internalization of movements.

When you have determined the rhythm for the class and which new skills to teach, **create your lesson plan** step-by-step including subjects, teaching methods and the amount of time for each subject.

3 Stages of the Lesson Plan

A typical lesson plan is created around the three stages of daily training:

1) Warm-up
2) Core Training
3) Cool-down

The function of the **Warm-up** period is to activate the body's circulation, to prepare the joints and muscles for activity, and to raise the body's core temperature. Ten or fifteen minutes is the most desirable amount of time for warming-up. (For a more detailed discussion of warming-up see Chapter 4: Conditioning)

The **core training** stage consists of skill development, strategy, and cognitive training.   Decide the intensity and amount of training based on your present situation. There are five significant elements included in the core training curriculum:

1) techniques and strategies
2) speed training
3) strength training
4) endurance training
5) integration of the above skills and mental training

Techniques and strategies include forms, arranged and free combat skills, footwork, weapons, concealment, rhythm, set-ups, etc. Teach new skills early in the class when students' concentration is high and their physical condition is fresh. This will ensure that they fully apply themselves to mastering new skills.

Once these new skills have been internalized, move on to speed, endurance and strength training. Each of these elements can be taught alone or in combination with others. For example, wind sprints emphasize speed and leg strength but add little to actual combat skills. On the other hand, performing as many front kicks as you can in one minute improves speed and endurance as well as kicking skills. When designing speed, strength and endurance drills, emphasize simplicity. Basic, linear skills are best. Performing complex skills for conditioning is likely to lead to injuries.

There are many skills to teach in the core training stage. Plan for the specific needs of your students. Think of the core training period as the main course. Core training will require 35 to 40 minutes of a 60 minute class.

The final stage, the **cool down**, period is a time for recovering the body's pre-exercise condition. It is necessary to give the body an intermediate stage between intensive activity and inactivity. Activities like slow stretching and movement exercises encourage circulation and assist in removing chemical build-up from the muscles. Without removing the accumulation of chemicals in the muscles, they will feel sore and stiff the next day. The cool down period is also an excellent time to calm down mentally and return to a relaxed state of mind. Allow 5 to 10 minutes for cool down.

Creating a Lesson Plan

1. Consider objectives

2. Select new skills to teach

3. Determine the order and intensity of skills

4. Determine the rhythm for the class

5. Create the lesson plan

   a. Warm-up

   b. Core training

   - techniques and strategies

   - speed training

   - strength training

   - endurance training

   - integration of mental and physical

   c. Cool-down

Sample Lesson Plan for a Beginner Class

1. Objectives:
   a. to improve the general level of fitness
   b. to introduce front kick and middle punch
   c. to teach two joint lock techniques for self-defense

2. Training intensity: low intensity (for beginners)

3. Curriculum
   a. stretching and conditioning exercises
   b. front kick, middle punch
   c. basic blocking, stances
   d. joint locking techniques
   e. meditation

4. Plan

   A. Warming -up (15 min.)
      a. Jumping jacks (20 reps)
      b. Joint loosening exercises (neck, shoulders, hips, knees)
      c. upper body stretching (3 kinds)
      d. lower body stretching (5 kinds)
      e. push-ups (20 reps)
      f. sit-ups (20 reps)
      g. sprints (5 reps)

   B. Core training (35 min.)
      a. teach front kick/middle punch
      b. student practice (group/individual)
      c. review front kick/middle punch - key points
      d. review basic blocks/stances (group)
      e. teach shoulder grab and arm grab defenses
      f. practice with partner
      g. review self-defense - key points

   C. Cool-down (10 min.)
      a. meditation and action visualization for new skills
      b. light stretching

The Learning Process

To teach effectively, you must first understand the learning process that takes place in the students each time new material is presented. By understanding human information processing, you can adapt your methods to take advantage of the natural learning process.

To teach a subject, you have to first bring the information to the student's attention. Attention in humans is controlled by the sensory register. The sensory register filters all incoming information and holds it for three to five seconds. In this brief time, the sensory register decides if the information requires further attention or is unimportant. For example, if you are waiting for a bus on a busy street, the sensory register dismisses the continuous stream of passing cars as insignificant, but when a large vehicle approaches, it alerts the brain that this deserves further attention. This is why you pay little attention to the passing cars, but jump up when the bus or a similar vehicle approaches.

A basic challenge of teachers is making information important enough for the sensory register to alert other parts of the brain. The sensory register gives priority attention to information by anticipating what will follow based on information stored in the long-term memory. (Niesser, 1976) So to gain the attention of your students, you have to **begin each new subject with a view toward influencing the sensory register in a positive way**. Create the perception of interest in your introduction and your students will take notice of what is to follow.

After you get the attention of the student, consider how he will process and organize the incoming information. Learning results from an interaction between the environmental stimulus (information) and a learner (one who processes and transforms the information).

Information is processed in steps or stages as follows:

1. Attending to the stimulus
2. Recognizing it
3. Transforming it into some type of mental representation
4. Comparing it with information already stored in the memory

5. Assigning meaning to it
6. Acting on it in some fashion (Miller, 1983)

Once the student gives attention to the incoming information as valuable, he attempts to recognize it and in the instance of physical movements, create a visual model in his mind. He then compares it with similar information he has already learned. Next, he files it in the correct place and takes action according to the situation. By understanding this process, we can see that **teaching progressively is important**. If you teach a new skill based on the previously learned skill, the student processes the new information easily because he has a ready comparison and a place in which to file the information. However, if you jump around and teach many different types of skills, the mental process is cumbersome and delays progress.

The information processing system is complex and therefor only small amounts of information can be processed at a time. **Teach new skills in small segments** to allow for comprehensive learning and efficient processing. If the students misses part of the skill, the segment of learning may be too large. Break it down further to allow for accurate processing. Learning is an interactive process between the student and teacher. Both must be receptive and sensitive to one another.

In addition to the information processing system, learning is affected by several mitigating factors:

1. Learner characteristics (skill level, previous knowledge, general interest)
2. Learner activities (operations performed by the learner during the task)
3. Nature of learning material (visual, written)
4. Nature of criterion (type of evaluation process)
(Bransford, 1979)

When you design activities, consider these learner and curricular components to facilitate ease of learning. If a student learns best through observing a model, provide good demonstrations. If a student is a slow learner, teach more slowly and with large amounts of supplementary activities. If a student does not take written tests well, provide the opportunity for physical or oral evaluations. Conversely, if a student is older and not physically adept, substitute a written thesis on the philosophy of your art for complex physical skills. **You must adapt to your students' learning style** or they will become frustrated and lose interest.

There is one additional aspect of learning that you must understand when you are planning your curriculum. **Transfer of learning** was first identified by Thorndike and Woodworth in 1901 and became known as the "Theory of Identical Elements." Their theory states that the greater the degree of similarity between tasks' stimulus and response elements, the greater the amount of transfer occurs. Simply stated, information stored in the brain greatly affects the learning of new yet similar information.

This became a much studied theory among behavioral scientists and led to the classification of three types of transfer: Positive, Negative and Zero transfer. **Positive transfer** is defined as a situation in which prior learning aids subsequent learning. A good example is a student who has already learned turn kick will easily learn jumping turn kick, because the action required for the two is similar.

Conversely, **negative transfer** is defined as a situation in which prior learning interferes with subsequent learning. In this case, the two tasks are highly similar but require different responses. If you teach front snap kick to a beginner he will learn it relatively quickly. However, when you then teach front pushing kick, he may experience some difficulty. Both kicks are called front kick and both require very similar physical movements, yet the required results are different. Front snap kick requires speed and agility. Front pushing kick requires power and gross motor coordination. When teaching different but similar skills, **emphasize the differences** rather than the similarities.

Finally, **zero transfer** is a situation in which prior learning has no effect on subsequent learning. For example, having previously learned front kick has no effect on memorizing the school rules. The two skills are entirely unrelated and the brain does not check one to process the other.

Effective Teaching Methods

For teaching to be meaningful, it has to be useful and effective. To meet these objectives, approach every class with a natural but disciplined attitude and with the intention to create a positive atmosphere in which learning can take place. The solution for effective teaching is to have a well-formulated approach. Devise and use a consistent method for teaching new skills.

Introduction of New Skills

An excellent way to introduce new skills is through the following five step approach. The first step is to **provide information** about the new skill. A brief introduction might include the situation in which to use the technique and a few key points about correct performance. By giving students an idea of what they will learn, you heighten their anticipation for learning. They also can begin to visualize what they must do to learn it.

The second stage is to **demonstrate the skill**. Demonstrate first at regular speed once or twice, then repeat the movement in slow motion several times. Demonstrate from different angles so the entire class can clearly see what you are doing. When you are certain everyone understands how to proceed, begin step three.

Break the technique into several parts. Each part should consist of one or two simple movements. For example, when teaching side kick to beginners, break it into six segments as follows:

1. Fighting stance
2. Raise the knee
3. Turn the hip and cock the kicking leg
4. Stretch out the leg
5. Pull the leg back to the cocked position
6. Return to fighting stance

As the student progresses, combine the segments logically. Using the same sidekick, combine the movements as follows:

1. Fighting stance
2. Raise the knee, turn the hips and stretch out the leg
3. Retract the leg
4. Return to fighting stance

As the student becomes proficient at this, teach him to kick in one fluid motion.

The fourth step is **application**. When the student understands how to execute the new technique, begin teaching simple applications. If he can perform the side kick well, show him the target areas which are vulnerable to the side kick such as the knee joint, rib cage, neck and head. You also can teach variations like front leg side kick, sliding in side kick, spinning side kick, etc.

The final and most important step in teaching a new skill is **practice and perfection**. Only practice can lead students to discover the intricacies of the technique. The ability to develop and adapt new skills is one of the most potent forces in keeping students interested in their martial arts practice.

Introduction of New Skills

1. Provide information about the skill.
2. Demonstrate the skill.
3. Break the skill into several parts.
4. Combine parts into one fluid movement.
5. Teach applications.
6. Allow the student to practice and perfect the skill.

Maintaining Student Interest

Maintaining student interest is a very demanding and critical area of teaching. Without interested students, who will you teach? Keeping students interested can be loosely interpreted as consistently keeping their attention. This can be difficult because attention spans vary from person to person, especially among children. You will need to develop a system for maintaining student interest in your classes.

Start with simplicity

In the beginner stage, a variety of simple activities are effective in providing fun and excitement. To motivate new students, realistic and sensible movements are better than monotonous drills. Start with exciting skills that are easy to understand and perform. Simplicity is especially important in group lessons because any complex cues from you might cause confusion. In a group situation, the student is less likely to voice his confusion and it will go unresolved. The more confusion a student experiences, the more likely he is to drop out.

As the student begins to show a genuine interest, start teaching individual movements with more precise explanations and positive feedback. Avoid negative criticism that might cause embarrassment or insecurity. Have patience and a positive attitude in the beginner stage. If there is even one good facet of a movement, encourage it.

Show your students the possibility for improvement. In learning, there are three possible responses to a new movement. In some cases, the student will adapt to the new skill right away with little or no transition time. At the other extreme, the student will become confused and frustrated and give up his effort to complete the skill. However, in most cases, the student will attempt to overcome his initial confusion and adjust his behavior to meet the demands of the new skill.

Strive to lead your students to adaptation or adjustment with every new skill you present. If a student becomes confused and makes mistakes, don't just say, "Don't do that!" Instead provide him with positive alternatives. Your positive encouragement will undoubtedly increase his effort and success.

Make a fire of success

To keep a student interested throughout the beginner stage, help him have as many successful experiences as possible. When succeeding becomes the norm in his training, he will try to increase the number of successes he has. Meanwhile, his unsuccessful experiences will gradually fade away.

Teaching a beginner is like trying to make a campfire in a field. If the wood is dry, it's easy to light the fire. If the wood is wet or the weather is too windy, it is difficult to start the fire and keep it burning. In this situation, you can put some dry branches or paper on even the smallest flame to make the fire grow. Too much wind or a log that is too big will quickly snuff out your hard work. It takes care and patience to get the fire burning. The same principle is true for catching the interest of a new student.

Once the fire catches, you can be bold and throw on some larger logs. Then sit back and relax for awhile, the fire will take care of itself with only occasional prompting. This is a good metaphor for the Intermediate stage of learning. You have to give students more and greater challenges to enhance the depth of their knowledge. Teach complex combinations, applications and strategies. View this as their preparation for the advanced stage. Provide reinforcement and feedback as well as careful reminders about errors and bad habits. The former encourages correctly performed movements to develop further. The latter provides the student with opportunities to expand his knowledge of his performance and to study the art in depth.

Fulfill extrinsic needs

During the intermediate period of learning, the student may begin to have an interest in the theory and history of the art he is learning. If you sense this, introduce some basic ideas to him. This will sustain him if he reaches a plateau or feels bored in his daily practice. Another way to deepen the intermediate student's interest is to allow him to take an active role in school events such as demonstrations and competitions. This will give him short term goals and provide him with an opportunity to gauge his current level of ability.

It is also at this time that students should be allowed to try many different patterns of practicing so that they can find the way that is best suited to their physical and emotional condition. As intermediate students experiment with different training methods, aim to give them proper feedback at the right time. If you give them too much feedback, you confine them. If you don't guide them, they may lose their way. Guide them gently in the right direction and allow them to learn from their mistakes. This process will give them a sense of progress and increase their intrinsic motivation. This is the best combination for successfully bringing students through the intermediate stage.

Fulfill intrinsic needs

At the advanced level, your students should already know what is important in martial arts and why they are training. Their purpose in training is no longer only physical. With this in mind, broaden their knowledge of philosophy, history, tradition, movement theory, etc. Advanced students know the importance of patience and step-by-step progress. Perfection of skills and self-exploration are priorities for them. In a word, what advanced students are looking for is depth. How well you keep your advanced students is a measure of your depth as an instructor.

Maintaining Student Interest

1. Beginner
a. Begin with a variety of simple skills
b. Teach in a straightforward manner
c. Provide positive reinforcement

2. Intermediate
a. Introduce history and philosophy
b. Individualize training methods
c. Increase intrinsic motivation by minimizing feedback

3. Advanced
a. Broaden knowledge through instructor training
b. Encourage perfection of skills and self-fulfillment
c. Provide opportunities to teach

Instructor Assessment Guide

You may find the following questions useful to assess your current teaching plan and identify ways to implement the ideas in this chapter as well as your own new ideas.

Fundamentals of teaching

1. What is the current general level of my students in terms of accepted standards?
   a. As compared with my expectations?
   b. As compared to other students in my geographic area?
   c. As compared with other students nationally in my art?

2. What areas do my students need to improve? *List at least three and identify methods of improvement that can be implemented today.*

3. How do I currently assess the ability of my students to meet accepted standards of performance?

4. How often do I make thorough assessments of each student?

Meeting Educational Goals

1. Do I reinforce effective work habits during practice time?

2. Do I encourage students to pursue long term goals, even though they may be difficult?

3. Do I teach students the proper use for their self-defense skills?

4. Do I encourage respect for partners and opponents during drills and practice?

5. Do I teach students the artistic, as well as practical, values of my art?

6. Do I encourage students to lead a healthy life-style?

7. Do I provide sound, practical advice regarding diet, fitness and exercise as guidelines for improvement?

Teaching Methodology

1. Do I adapt my teaching style to meet my students learning styles?

2. Do I allow for individual differences within the framework of a structured curriculum?

3. Do I present new skills clearly in a consistent manner?

4.Do I teach skills progressively, relating new skills to familiar tasks?

5. Do I break skills into segments for ease of learning?

6. Do I set clear, attainable objectives for individual students?

7. Do I set clear short and long-term goals for each class as a group?

Classroom Management

1. Does the class have clearly defined rules of acceptable behavior?

2. Do students know what is expected of them during class time?

3. Are students free from confusion and distraction?

4. What type of atmosphere currently exists in my classes, competitive or cooperative?

5. How can I best take advantage of this atmosphere?

6. Is this atmosphere damaging to the students learning process?

7. Are students primarily intrinsically or extrinsically motivated?

8. How I can further encourage intrinsic motivation?

9. What types of extrinsic motivation works best?

10. How frequently do I provide extrinsic motivation?

Evaluation

1. Do I regularly make a written analysis of my teaching performance?

2. Do I truly examine the faults of my teaching?

3. Have I made a sincere effort to improve deficient areas?

4. What are the objectives of student testing?

5. Do I analyze current performance levels and make general as well as individual plans for improvement?

15 Tips for Effective Teaching

1. Start class with simple and exciting activities

2. Simplify your commands. Ask students to perform one task at a time.

3. Give specific physical cues when you teach a new skill.

4. After a technique becomes fluent, provide the student with strategy related cues rather than skill related cues.

5. Teach variations to meet a variety of situations.

6. Teach effective strategies and tactics to improve your students' insight into the art.

7. Detect and correct errors as soon as they occur.

8. Organize practice sessions so learning is progressive.

9. Provide feedback when necessary and guide students toward long-term results.

10. Encourage positive aspects of performance whenever possible.

11. Reward students who perform exceptionally well.

12. Motivate students toward consistent workouts and achievements.

13. Communicate with students on both verbal and nonverbal levels.

14. Be patient. Try to find the diamond in the rough.

15. Be an innovator. Everyone favors new, exciting ideas over dull routines.

Professionalism in Teaching

The final subject in this chapter is how to communicate with your students in a class setting. No matter how trivial this might seem, it is a subject you cannot neglect. What you say and how you say it will make up a large part of your students' impression of you.

Most importantly, don't talk too much. If you spend half the class talking, your students have to spend half the class listening. They are coming to you to learn a physical discipline that comes from practice, not discussion. But don't be afraid to talk when you have something pertinent to say. Provide adequate verbal feedback to let your students know that you are tuned in to them. Strive to strike a balance between ample student practice, competent demonstrations and proper explanations.

When you explain something, simplify what you want to say and get to the point. If your explanation is about a new skill, make sure most of the class understands it and move on. No matter how well you explain things, there will always be people who don't understand. Don't be overly concerned about this. Spend time with them during the practice time that follows your demonstration.

When you address the class, keep your voice firm and sincere. When you talk to your students, your voice will tell them who you really are. When you teach, be yourself. Before you speak, carefully consider what you need to convey to students. In class, your subject should be confined to the art. The only reason for you to talk is to improve your students abilities and to enhance their knowledge.

Though you are serious and commanding in the class, talk to students gently and with respect outside of class. You can be a drill sergeant in the training hall, but be a gentleman or woman in person. The harmony of the two extremes is the result of proper training. Students will learn from your attitude that you are very serious in training and you are a good human being. This is the attitude of a winner.

This balance of seriousness and sincerity takes time and effort to achieve. Practice at every opportunity. Through practicing how to speak, you will gain very solid confidence in your speech and voice. Soon you will deliver exactly what you want to express to your students. More surprisingly, you will do it without preparation. You will become a natural speaker. This will make your teaching smoother and your students at ease with your teaching style.

Through trial and error, you will learn many new things about yourself and your students. But you will never know unless you try. You will be amazed by your ability. Try it. Soon you will find yourself to be the master of speech, of teaching, of the art and most of all, of your potential. You are the student of your teaching. This is the way of a great teacher.

Maintaining a Professional Demeanor

1. Be firm and authoritative in disciplining students.
2. Be persuasive in explaining new skills.
3. Be informative in teaching philosophy and history.
4. Be kind and polite when questioned by students.
5. Be prepared for class.
6. Avoid talking about personal matters.
7. Keep the balance of seriousness and sincerity.

Management

*Benefiting others is truly
the foundation of
benefiting oneself.*

- Hung Ying-Ming

Chapter 6
Student Management

In a martial art school, the term student management denotes guiding students as a dynamic and hard working unit to achieve predetermined objectives. Successful management involves working both with and through your students toward the achievement of mutual goals. By knowing the direction in which your students are moving, you can make successful decisions in your school. Observe your students. Listen carefully to their concerns and comments. Based on the information that you receive directly or indirectly from the students, you can make decisions and initiate actions that strengthen your school.

You are responsible for the direction of your school and for providing quality teaching. Besides these major responsibilities, there are many other facets of management to consider including scheduling classes, budgeting, public relations, evaluation and student counseling. This chapter, however, focuses on the teaching aspects of student management.

To be a good teacher, it is necessary to have the ability to manage students with sound professional knowledge. Your job is to remove the obstacles your students face so they can see and achieve their goals. Help them meet and overcome challenges by themselves so they can mature and gain self-confidence. As they achieve their goals, the goals of your school also will be realized. It is important to recognize that every individual student is part of the powerful force that drives your school forward. Therefore, actively promote the positive contributions of each individual.

Classroom Management

Deft management is an integral part of teaching. How you manage your school atmosphere determines how your students perceive your teaching skills. A **well managed classroom** is identified by four characteristics:

1. Students know what they are expected to do and are generally successful at it.
2. Students are busy in teacher led activities.
3. There is minimal waste of time, confusion or disruption.
4. A no-nonsense, work oriented tone prevails but there is a relaxed pleasant atmosphere.

(Brophy, 1979, Good, 1982)

The first three are directly related to your ability to accurately set clear objectives and to plan a course of action. However, number four is perhaps the most difficult and deficient area for martial arts instructors. Many instructors create a work oriented tone in their school, but few can combine it with a pleasant atmosphere. Often the atmosphere is tense and harsh. Punishment is meted out frequently and junior students are subjected to the demands of their seniors without regard for their welfare.

This is an atmosphere that must be consigned to the history books if the martial arts are to become an accepted means of education. Successful instructors are the ones who make training enjoyable and rewarding for students. Enjoyable and pleasant should not be confused with fun. They connote a feeling of wanting to attend class and of truly liking training as a means of self-fulfillment. This is why pursuits like chess and piano playing are so widely practiced. They require hard work and dedication, but they also provide the practitioner with a pleasant sense of accomplishment.

So how can an instructor provide his students with an atmosphere they will like and respect? Basically there are four types of **class management techniques**:

1. Individual competition

Only a small number of students can gain the greatest rewards and only at the expense of others. *Example:* Only the top five test applicants are promoted to black belt and all others fail.

2. Individual reward

All rewards/achievements are independent of other students. *Example:* Students test for black belt based on their level of skill and all students who meet the set criteria pass.

3. Group competition

Groups of students compete with other groups for available rewards. *Example:* The group who learns their form the fastest receives a rest period.

4. Group reward

Rewards are given on the basis of the quality of the groups' performance independent of other groups. *Example:* All groups who learn their form during the allotted time receive a rest period.

Which structure you implement depends on the results you are trying to achieve. Cooperative learning (group reward and individual reward) leads to success in classroom tasks, a high degree of commitment to learning, curiosity about new subjects and high intrinsic motivation. On the other hand, competitive learning (individual competition and group competition) leads to low expectations for success, low commitment to learning, lack of persistence, a "winners vs. losers" atmosphere, the avoidance of failure through nonparticipation, low effort and low levels of aspiration. (Johnson & Johnson, 1974, 1978) Competitive learning should only be utilized when all members of the class are able to compete effectively. If some students are obviously disadvantaged, they become easily discouraged and resent your teaching methods.

Once you have established your primary classroom structure, work toward guiding your students to successful experiences and a positive self-concept. Let them know that you are **in charge** of the class and aware of what is going on in the classroom at all times. Maintain **smoothness** in your teaching to **create a momentum** that propels the class forward. Provide a **variety of activities** and show your enthusiasm for learning to your students. Above all, demonstrate your preparedness and **competence** in your art regularly. If your students perceive you as knowledgeable, they will follow your instructions readily.

Cooperative learning =

success, commitment, motivation, curiosity

Competitive learning =

high expectations, low commitment, lack of participation

Student Grouping

Because of the variability among students, teachers must precisely consider how to organize classes to best accelerate learning. There are four commonly accepted ways of grouping students:

1. Between class ability grouping

Each class is made up of students homogeneous in one ability/skill. *Example*: All junior red belts

2. Regrouping

Students are narrowly grouped by age and ability in one subject. *Example*: Red belts age 14 to 16 skilled in sparring

3. Joplin Plan

Students at the same level regardless of age are grouped together. *Example*: All red belts

4. Within class grouping

Divide the class into smaller groups according to ability to practice a specific skill. *Example*: Small groups among red belts according to their highest form

The Joplin Plan and within class grouping have been shown to have superior results because the groups are ability driven and a variety of age levels interact to produce varied group personalities. Martial arts classes are often unique because they allow people of different ages and education levels to blend together in one class. The instructor can use this to his advantage by encouraging students who are older or more highly educated to assist students who are below average in ability.

Teaching Children

Growth is an ongoing process and children differ in every stage of their growth. For this reason, you have to establish a program to meet the needs of all children. Include a variety of activities and experiences that will help young students form a solid foundation on which to build more complex techniques and knowledge. If children concentrate on making their basics strong when they are young, they will quickly learn advanced skills as they mature physically.

Make your program for children progressive and developmental. This is the component of martial arts that many parents are particularly interested in for their children. Consider the developmental age groups of children as you plan your class activities.

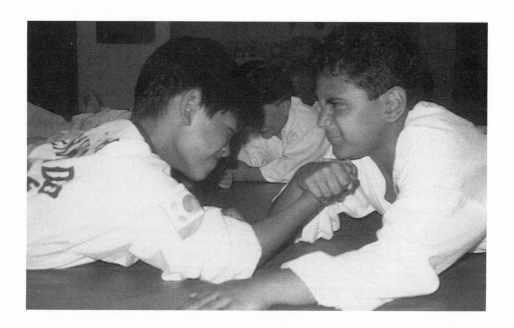

3 to 6 Years Old

Characteristics:
1. Extremely active and curious; prone to bursts of activity
2. Very flexible and resilient both physically and mentally
3. Good control of major muscle groups
4. Searching for limits on behavior
5. Enjoy encouragement and appreciation

Teaching Emphasis on:
1. Simple, exciting activities followed by periods of rest or quiet activities
2. Activities that encourage basic physical skills like coordination, balance, following directions, etc.
3. Skills that develop major muscle groups like running, jumping, kicking, punching, etc.
4. Firm discipline through consistent enforcement of clearly defined rules (especially safety rules)
5. Encourage effort and cooperation more than results.

6 to 9 Years Old

Characteristics:
1. Very active, but confined by demands of school
2. Aggression becoming more prominent
3. Concerned with rules and organization
4. Great physical confidence but overestimate abilities (accident rate peaks at 9)
5. Eager to please teachers, admire teachers
6. Sensitive to criticism, difficulty handling failure
7. Strong desire for knowledge

Teaching Emphasis on:
1. Active participation followed by rest periods
2. Rough activities like light bag kicking to disperse aggression
3. Small group games (cooperative) with simple rules
4. Strict limits on acceptable behavior, especially during free practice periods
5. Appoint helpers or leaders for each class to encourage leadership
6. Avoid criticism, provide many opportunities for success in the classroom
7. Vary class from day to day and present skills in different ways

9 to 12 Years Old

Characteristics
1. Growth spurt in girls and some boys
2. Fine motor coordination developing
3. Peer group acceptance replacing adults as role model
4. Competitiveness, desire for recognition high
5. Establishing identity separate from parents

Teaching Emphasis on:
1. Design competitive activities with sex/size/strength differences in mind
2. Teach skills in more detail and with higher difficulty levels (including timing, reflexes, coordination, etc.)
3. Small group activities to encourage both cooperation and competition between groups
4. Contests and games (races, arm wrestling, speed target kicking) that yield several winners. Vary games so everyone has a chance to win. Encourage competition in local events if students have interest.
5. Encourage responsible behavior and goal setting. Provide opportunities for self directed learning

12 to 15 Years Old

Characteristics:
1. Growth spurt begins in boys; great concern about physical appearance in both sexes
2. Girls excel in flexibility and balance; boys excel in strength, speed and endurance due to large body structure and greater heart/lung capacity
3. Peer group acceptance is a top priority
4. Self-image is taking shape
5. Attention span lengthens
6. Ability for sustained aerobic activity developed

Teaching emphasis on:
1. Avoid criticism, especially of physical faults
2. Encourage strengths, compensate for weaknesses
3. Encourage cooperative activities that demand problem solving, creativity for success
4. Give ample positive feedback and teach the student how to improve and excel
5. Begin teaching complex skills that require lengthy practice
6. Encourage the student to compete at high levels (national) if he is interested and able

Depending on the number of children you teach, you can break up the classes as you see fit. There should be at least two separate age groups (4-8, 9-12). With a large number of children, you can divide them by skill level as well. As youths reach adolescence, most will feel more comfortable in an adult class. When their attention span lengthens and they reach physical maturity, they will enjoy the challenge of learning adult skills.

When you organize your junior classes, provide age appropriate activities in each class. This heightens student interest and maintain it over a long period. In addition to age appropriateness, consider safety in your planning. Children are always at risk of injury and need to be vigilantly supervised. Set strict rules for safety and explain to the children why they have to follow them.

In summary, make your classes for children fun, exciting, safe and educational.

Teaching Adults

Adults, like children, have many characteristics inherent to their age. When you plan adult classes, remember that adults are unique in many ways. Use the following guidelines to improve your adult classes.

1. Adults are prone to muscle and joint stiffness throughout the beginner and intermediate stages. Provide adequate warming up, stretching, and conditioning exercises in every class.

2. Adults are at high risk for joint and muscle injuries, especially as they advance in age. Take caution in teaching skills that stress the joints and muscles. Prepare the required muscles well through conditioning exercises.

3. Adult beginners are often self-conscious. Reassure them that everyone has to start somewhere and effort is most important for improvement.

4. Many adults have firmly established habits and value systems. Do not enforce philosophy or ideas in your teaching. Present new concepts intelligently and let the students accept them at their own pace.

5. Adults need relief from the stress and demands of their daily life. Remove the feeling of routineness by varying the content and structure of the class regularly. Make your class an opportunity for them to regenerate their energy.

Coping with Disruptive Students

Students who intentionally disrupt the class require strict discipline and conduct standards. They need and want a person who can provide them with the stability and security they lack in their lives. You are the person who can provide the strong, positive influence they are looking for. To do this, treat them as you treat other students. Do not treat them as troublemakers. If they have a reputation of being a troublemaker, they are used to living up to their reputation. You can break this cycle by expecting them to conform to the same behavior as the rest of the class.

In general, people who habitually cause problems are insecure. These people will try to test your authority, hoping not to get caught. Or they might openly defy you and hope that you are incapable of handling their behavior. The best way to deal with rebellious students is to set the rules and establish order before you begin to teach. Then they know what to do and what is expected of them.

It is important to deal with a problem in the class when it arises. If you ignore the person who initiated the problem, they will do it again soon. If you appear helpless in a discipline situation, students will feel insecure and lose respect for you. If you handle discipline confidently and strongly, even the most difficult students will want to continue learning. Ironically, one of your most difficult white belts may turn out to be one of your best black belts in the future. It's up to you.

There are several principles for disciplining students. Most importantly, **the rules of the school must be clear and have a definite purpose**. Every student should understand the reasons for the rules and that any violation of the rules wastes time and may result in punishment. Enforce the rules consistently. If a change in procedure becomes necessary, phase it in gradually. The fewer changes that take place in the classroom rules and structure, the more secure students feel.

When you correct a student, speak firmly but softly. Do not humiliate him or attack him personally. Instead focus your correction on the improper behavior. Identify the infraction clearly and suggest an appropriate alternative behavior. If the misbehavior continues, it may be helpful to remind the student that everything he does in class directly affects his progress and his eligibility for promotion.

Knowing when to discipline students is as important as knowing how to discipline them. Take immediate action when the situation warrants it. However, there are times when the interruption is minor and giving your full attention to the rest of the class is more beneficial. If you feel it is necessary, speak to the offending student later, such as after class.

If you choose to ignore disruptive behavior, make sure the behavior is not being reinforced by other members of the class. Sometimes ignoring minor behavior causes it to disappear. But if a student's behavior draws the attention of the class away from you, it is being reinforced and needs to be actively stopped.

The best way to handle disruptive behavior is to prevent it from happening. Keep your instruction clear and concise. Make your students' minds active and occupied. Provide positive feedback for positive behavior. Actively incorporate preventive discipline in your curriculum maintaining your standards in spite of the changes of environment caused by disruptive students.

Handling disruptive students

1. Make school rules clear and with a definite purpose.

2. Speak firmly, but softly when correcting students.

3. Know when to discipline students.

4. Implement preventive discipline in your curriculum.

Exceptional Students

In a balanced classroom environment, there are many talented students and many slow learners. If you focus on one extreme or the other, you will lose many students along the way. Inexperienced instructors have a tendency to favor the talented students and give them special attention. If you do this, the average and slow students will feel inadequate and left out. Conversely, if you give too much attention to the slower students, others will feel bored and uninterested.

In daily classes, adjust the pace to the average, middle level students. To keep the interest of all students including those who are ahead of or behind the median, plan a well harmonized class including simple as well as difficult skills and fun as well as challenging activities.

Talented Students

Talented students need additional, specific guidelines to help them reach their full potential. Occasionally teach them individually before or after class to improve their personal strengths. In class, provide them with detailed feedback. Set high goals and push them to their limit. Achieving goals is a form of self-discipline, which is very important for talented athletes. If they progress to the top competition levels, they will need good self-discipline to go the extra distance it takes to win.

At the advanced stage, provide them with the knowledge and equipment they need to improve independently. Audio-visual materials are very helpful in this regard. Video taping a students performance and allowing him to watch it can improve the detailed aspects of his movements. Keep in mind that an above average student may become a prominent martial artist who may enhance the level of martial arts in the future.

However, be cautious in encouraging talented students. Many naturally gifted athletes lack endurance. They know that they are better than others and that they can excel with relatively little effort. This attitude often materializes as arrogance. You have to differentiate correctly between pride and arrogance. The former respects self and others; the latter respects neither. The former is positive and the latter is negative. Since martial art practice is aimed at developing positive attitudes, teach your students the difference between the two. To avoid arrogance, help talented students concentrate on developing their intrinsic talents for self-fulfillment.

Video taping your performance can provide valuable feedback on advanced skills.

Slow Learners

For those students at the other extreme, the slow learners, be patient. Be sensitive in talking to them because any negative comments on their performance or ability discourage them. Treat them just as you treat your average students. When they cannot perform a certain movement, encourage them to perform to their personal best. For them, the key is to keep trying, to have consistent guidelines and to learn skills step-by-step. Never let them skip a level of learning because they can easily get lost.

Reassure your slower students that everyone must start somewhere to improve. Whether you are talented really does not matter. Without starting from the beginning, you cannot become an expert. How much you improve is more important than where you began.

An excellent example of this is a student who joined my school several years ago. When she started training, she found that the movements and techniques did not come naturally for her. Instead of giving up, she accepted this and resolved to overcome her difficulties. She practiced consistently and worked harder than many other students. As she began to catch up with the average students, she was in the habit of pushing herself and continued to do so. This consistent effort allowed her to reach her goals including winning in competition and achieving her black belt. Not only did she learn to excel physically, but she became a dedicated and serious student of the martial arts.

In life, how hard you consistently try is more powerful than what you have to start with. If you set a goal to improve to a certain level and cease your efforts when you reach it, this is your limitation. But, if you don't have the limitation of "how much" or "how soon", your potential is boundless. Instill this in your students. Let them be free from limitations and see the endless possibilities of the human spirit.

Teach slower student the fundamentals of your art. Urge them to practice basics repeatedly. Through repetition, they will build skill and confidence. Without learning complex skills, they can still participate fully in classes or competitions. Their success will depend on your ability to choose the correct skills to teach them.

Without self-limitation, your potential is boundless.

Special Interest Classes

When students complete their beginner and intermediate training courses, they may find they have developed special needs or interests. If this is the case with many students at your school, organize some special classes or seminars. The purpose of a special interest class is to improve specific skills in which the participants are especially interested or talented. The most popular special interest classes are sparring, forms, self-defense and history/philosophy. You can also try topics such as breaking, weapons, diversified arts, refereeing, and instructor training.

When designing a special interest class, keep in mind that the participants have high expectations. To meet these expectations, special interest classes must be intensive and individualized. The training methods for special classes should be different from those of the regular classes. In a special interest class, the quality of training is the focal point.

To develop specific skills, the student must practice correctly and at a high level of intensity. The more they practice, the more perfect their skills will become. As they near perfection in crucial skills, their techniques reach maximum efficiency. This is usually the student's main goal when he decides to join a special class. If your teaching is accurate, the student will see marked improvement and his expectations will be fulfilled.

Special interest classes don't have to be long term or permanent. It is most effective to have a maximum of six to eight weeks of intensive training in one subject to avoid burnout. By intensive training, I do not mean nonstop intensity in every class. Arrange the class so students have sufficient rest and recovery periods. When students are fatigued they cannot improve and the likelihood of injury is increased.

At the beginning of the session, assess each individual's character and ability. Observe the students carefully and provide them with accurate feedback. Because special classes are smaller than regular classes, students expect to receive more personalized teaching. When the special class unit is completed, the participants should have a significantly deeper understanding of the topic than they did before. They should also have a clear idea of what the next step in their training will be. Provide each special class student with at least one new challenge for them to tackle when they return to their regular training schedule.

When planning a special class begin with a list of objectives. Some goals that are influential in planning special interest classes are:

1. to build the student's confidence in his performance
2. to promote balanced physical development
3. to develop special abilities such as reflexes, strength, speed, power and stamina
4. to strengthen mental endurance
5. to prepare for competition
6. to enhance internal appreciation for the art
7. to gain practical knowledge and experience
8. to be exposed to a new area of the art

As a guide for your special classes, I have included three sample plans for forms, sparring and self-defense classes. Based on these, design your special classes and seminars.

Forms Class

1. Objectives
   a. Improve the coordination, balance, speed, and power control of the student.
   b. Find the perfect stances for each individual to give him mobility and stability.
   c. Enable each student to perform correctly and with proper understanding of the meaning of the form.
   d. Instill in the student the ability to appreciate the beauty of human movements.

2. Number of Participants
   a. 12 to 15 students
   b. Participants must be blue belt or above

3. Class Schedule
   a. July 7th to September 7th
   b. Wednesday, 7:00 to 8:00 PM

4. Teaching Methods
   a. Large group practice to master timing
   b. Small group practice to correct individual movements
   c. Individual practice to improve precision movements an enhance inner understanding
   d. Practice in front of a mirror to perfect the angle and position of movements
   e. Observe the performance of others to develop insight into the evaluation and comparison of forms
   f. Perform in front of the instructor or video camera for an in depth review of performance

5. Equipment
   a. mirror
   b. video camera and T.V. for self-analysis (optional)

Sparring Class

1. Objectives
   a. Improve speed, timing reflexes, and agility to enhance free sparring ability.
   b. Sharpen the mental and physical awareness of the students.
   c. Enhance the endurance level of the students.
   d. Develop the mentality needed for competition.

2. Number of Participants
   a. 8 to 12 students
   b. Students need instructor's approval

3. Class Schedule
   a. March 3rd to May 3rd
   b. Thursday, 7:00 to 9:00 PM

4. Teaching Methods
   a. Stretching exercises - 25 kinds
   b. Shuttle running - 5 sets
   c. Knee-touch jumping - 20 times
   d. Push-ups/sit-ups - 100 each
   e. Jumping rope - 3 three minute rounds
   f. Footwork training - 10 minutes
   g. Target kicking - 10 minutes
   h. Moving target drills - 10 minutes
   i. Heavy bag work - 10 minutes
   j. Arranged sparring w/partner - 10 minutes
   k. Free combinations - 10 minutes
   l. Free sparring - 3 rounds

5. Equipment
   a. targets and mitts
   b. heavy bag
   c. jump ropes
   d. protection gear
   e. stopwatch

Self-defense Class

1. Objectives
   a. Give the students a complete understanding of the psychology of self-defense.
   b. Develop the ability to mobilize the body efficiently in a dangerous situation.
   c. Give the students knowledge of specific techniques for specific situations.
   d. Prepare the student's mind and body for the reality of a self-defense encounter.

2. Number of Participants
   a. 16 to 20 students
   b. Students must be green belt or above

3. Class Schedule
   a. October 1st to December 1st
   b. Monday, 7:00 to 8:30 PM

4. Teaching Methods
   a. Practice blocking, striking, kicking, locking techniques.
   b. Practice case by case methods of defense.
   c. Improve reflexes by repeated practice of skills.
   d. Improve the ability to judge the seriousness of situation.

5. Equipment
   a. protection gear (as necessary)
   b. kicking dummy or heavy bag

Reducing Dropouts

If you implement all of the recommendations in this chapter, your dropout rate is likely to decrease. However, no matter how well you teach and how skillfully you manage your students, people will leave regularly. Let's examine the possible reasons for dropouts and what you can do to prevent them.

1. Dropouts Due to Instructor's Actions

A. Unfair/disrespectful treatment of students
- Treat all students equally
- Reconsider your attitude toward students
- Acknowledge the individuality of everyone

B. Lack of knowledge or experience
- Study continuously
- Project a professional image
- Analyze weakness and how to improve

C. Personality/character clash with student
- Accept individual differences
- Seek compromise in your behavior

D. Major change in school policy
- Make changes gradually
- Inform students well ahead of time
- Use student/parent surveys to assess needs

E. Improper balance of discipline
- Reconsider disciplinary needs of students
- Reconsider appropriateness of rules

2. Dropouts Due to Students' Actions

A. Problem with other students
  • Joint counseling to solve differences
  • Place students in separate classes

B. Student injured while training
  • Counsel student during recovery time
  • Provide alternative training methods
  • Reconsider intensity/content of classes

C. Student unsatisfied with training
  • Analyze needs/expectations with student
  • Reset goals

D. Lack of motivation; boredom
  • Give personal challenge
  • Help to make strong self-commitment

E. Student unable to keep up with class
  • Move to easier class
  • Give private lessons to catch up
  • Reduce difficulty level of class

3. Reasons Not Related to Training

A. Student has financial difficulty
- Adjust payment plan

B. Non-martial arts related injury
- Provide alternative training/study
- Plan to train around injury

C. Student moving away
- Help to locate school in new community
- Create positive parting atmosphere

D. Student undergoes major life change
- Incorporate training into new life-style
- Reduce amount of training time

E. Student has change in priorities
- Indicate value of martial art in his life
- If no solution, leave the door open for the future

Through your effort and sensitivity, you can prevent many students from dropping out. The key is to make training a high priority in their life. Remind them of the positive effects of training. However, if you see that they have really lost interest or training is not what they really need at the present time, do not pressure them. Part with an open mind because they are still your student and perhaps some day they will regain their interest and come back again.

Building camaraderie among students contributes to a positive atmosphere in class and helps reduce dropouts.

Supplementary Training

*Look for knowledge not in
books but in things
themselves.*

- William Gilbert

CHAPTER 7
Supplementary Training Methods

Up to this point, this book has focused on skillful teaching and class management, the two key factors that make a successful martial arts instructor. This chapter includes the activities and knowledge that can further enhance your teaching ability. These supplementary training methods can be very helpful in motivating your students, but they are not necessary for the maintenance of your school. Special events like competition, demonstrations and outdoor training can all provide valuable experiences for the participants.

The use of special events and equipment are strong incentives for students to deepen their knowledge and become more intensely involved in the martial arts. They also provide the student with the chance to interact with other martial artists. Every year, millions of martial artists participate in competitions, demonstrations and training camps on every level from the regional to the international arena. These events foster goodwill and fellowship among martial artists and improve the quality of martial arts around the world.

To plan a special activity, consider the needs of your students and the available budget. Once you determine these needs, establish the goals for the program. To make your event a success, prepare well in advance and enlist the help of senior students if necessary. In this chapter are some suggestions to enable you to successfully use supplementary training methods as a way to improve the quality of your teaching.

Competition

Competition allows the student to evaluate his ability in a one-on-one match with an opponent of a similar skill level. It is also good motivation for the student to sharpen his skills. Knowing that he will test his abilities in front of a crowd of spectators is a powerful reason for pushing himself to the limit of his potential.

The experience of competition is unforgettable. The few minutes spent in the ring are like a compression of the competitor's life as a martial artist up to that point. When he win, he will feel proud and confident. When he loses, he will become more analytic about himself. After all, winning or losing does not matter as long as the competitor learns from his experience.

Instill this in your students when they compete. Before a competition, remind them that the outcome of the tournament cannot be used as a measuring stick for their value as a martial art student. Competition cannot change what the student has already achieved, it can only enlighten him as to how he can improve.

When your students decide that they want to compete, teach them the skills they need to perform well. Explain the rules, standards and procedures of the tournament. Be certain you are correctly informed of the rules because many promoters alter rules to suit their tournament. If you send a student to a tournament where the rules are poorly enforced, he could be injured or receive an unfair judgment as a result. In either case, he would almost certainly lose some interest in the martial arts.

Remind your students of the importance of their safety in competition. Never allow them to risk their health to compete. A tournament lasts only one day, but a serious injury can jeopardize the future of their training.

Once your students decide to attend a tournament, begin preparing them for the competition day. In most major tournaments there are two areas of competition - sparring and individual performance events. Each event requires rigorous preparation by the competitor. You can assist in their preparation by following the guidelines in this section.

Sparring

For sparring competition, a competitor should start preparing two months to one year in advance depending on the level and style of the competition. For a local tournament, a couple of months of intensive training is enough for the average student. For a regional competition, two to six months of preparation is required. For a national or international level competition at least one year of training is necessary. A training plan for competition should include fundamental physical training, sport-specific physical training and technical practice

Fundamental physical training consists of activities that help the athlete reach his optimal physical condition such as weight training, running, aerobics, etc. At the beginning of the training program, devote about 70% of the time to conditioning and 30% to repetitive practice of basic skills. This conditioning program should be followed for at least four to eight weeks before beginning sport-specific training.

In martial arts, **sport-specific training** means the conditioning of muscles that are predominantly used in the art in which the competitor is training. A typical martial arts sport-specific training program consists of interval training, stretching, footwork and weight training for the leg and abdomen muscles. At this stage, the proportion of conditioning and technical development is about fifty-fifty.

After one to two months of sport-specific conditioning, begin to focus on **technical practice** based on the physical condition that the athlete has achieved. At this time, about 30% of each workout is allotted for maintaining the athlete's optimal conditioning level. Seventy percent of practice time is spent for the perfection of skills. Free-sparring practice, target drills to improve accuracy and reflexes, and heavy bag workouts are important parts of technical practice.

The final stage in preparing for competition is establishing **mental fitness and individual strategy**. To improve the competitor's mental fitness, instill in him indomitable confidence and focus. This will enable him to execute his strategy without fear or hesitation. To develop an individual strategy, examine his strengths in terms of offensive and defensive skills. Focus on a few key skills.

On the day of the competition, instruct your students to arrive early to complete their registration and weigh-in. Assign an assistant coach to each competitor to support him throughout the competition. The coach's job is to help the competitor warm-up thoroughly before his match and to remind him of his planned strategy at the start of each contest. If the strategy fails in any way, the coach can encourage the competitor to rely on his training to regain the advantage in the match.

A coach also can assist the competitor by analyzing his opponent's strategy and giving him feedback for the next round or match. If the fighter is showing a particular weakness, the coach should correct it at the first opportunity. However, he should take care not to overwhelm his competitor with feedback. His priority is to help his fighter stay relaxed and secure throughout the competition.

After a match, the coach's responsibility is to help his competitor recover his condition as quickly as possible so he will be ready for the next match. If the competitor is too tired or has been injured, his coach can consult with the tournament coordinator, referee, or medical staff. He can then use his best judgment in allowing the fighter to continue or advising him to withdraw. This is a very serious decision because his advice greatly affects his competitor's emotional and physical well-being.

1 Year Training Plan			
Time	Conditioning		Skills
	Fund. PT	SS PT	Tech. Practice
0 - 3 mo.	off-season		(maintain flex./end.)
3 - 6 mo.	70%	—	30%
6-9 mo.	25%	25%	50%
9-12 mo.	—	30%	70%

A realistic training plan will lead to success in sparring competition.

Individual Performance Events

The second major area of competition is individual performance events. These events include forms (empty hand and weapons), self-defense and breaking. The judging and performance criteria for these events are similar.

The key elements of a performance that judges consider include:

1. Correct execution of movements
2. Correct stance and posture
3. Level of skills presented
4. Smooth transitions between movements
5. Successful completion of the performance
6. Confident kiai/kihap
7. Eye direction and eye contact
8. Overall impression of the performance
9. Confidence and attitude of the performer

Different judges and tournaments place more emphasis on certain areas of performance, but if you cover these areas thoroughly and knowledgeably in practice, your competitors have an excellent chance of scoring well. For more information on the technical aspects of teaching individual skills you can refer to Chapter 4.

Beyond technical performance, the judges are interested in the student's attitude and demeanor. Teach your competitors the correct etiquette for the competition area. In addition to respecting the judges and referees, teach your competitors to respect their opponents by congratulating the winners or if they win, acknowledging the good performance of their opponents. Win or lose, they should maintain the self-respect they have worked hard to attain.

Intraschool Competition

To promote healthy competition, you can hold an annual or semiannual school tournament. This is especially exciting when you have several schools because you can give prizes for interschool competition as well. A school-run tournament encourages less confident students to compete because they know that the rules are fair and familiar. They also have a good idea who their opponents will be because only school members are allowed to participate. For detailed information on how to plan and run a martial arts tournament, see the special report *Hosting a Successful Martial Arts Tournament* (Turtle Press, 1995).

Intraschool competition gives your advanced students the chance to sharpen their refereeing and management skills. Your beginning students can familiarize themselves with a tournament atmosphere. Also, parents and relatives will have the chance to see their family members compete and win. Consider having a cook-out or party after the tournament for students and their families to encourage interest and participation in the school.

While it is excellent to encourage competition for interested students, never overemphasize the importance of competition in your regular classes. Your students have many different reasons for learning a martial art. Present them with the option to compete as a way of improving themselves. This is the ultimate goal of martial art competition.

Intraschool competition is an excellent learning experience for young students.

Demonstrations

There are two reasons for putting on a public demonstration of your art - to promote your art through public education and to entertain spectators. If you do both well, you will provide an exciting demonstration and gain new students at the same time. This is beneficial for both your school and the audience.

When you accept an invitation to put on a demonstration, plan in advance. Decide the length of the demonstration, the number of participants, the equipment needed and the content of the demonstration. Rehearse at least once with all of the students involved to ensure a successful and safe demonstration.

A demonstration for a general interest audience should focus on the fundamental elements of the art - forms, breaking, self-defense, weapons, etc. If you are performing for a group that has a specific interest in one area, plan your demonstration accordingly. For example, if you are performing for a group of children, feature your young students because children relate well to one another. If you are performing for a women's group interested in self-defense, feature your female students of all ranks successfully defending themselves. If you are performing for law enforcement officials, stick to realistic skills with an emphasis on self-defense.

Plan to arrive at the demonstration site at least 15 minutes early. Assemble your students in an orderly manner and remind them that they are representing their school and their art. Emphasize that the school rules continue to apply until the demonstration is over. Assign several senior students to help the team warm-up and prepare for their performance.

While your students are preparing, survey the demonstration area. Check the size of the stage to ascertain that you have enough space for the activities you have planned. If the area is too small, secure more space or alter your plan accordingly. Check the surface of the area (grass, wood, concrete, mats) so you can advise the students of necessary precautions.

Begin the demonstration with simple and exciting performances. Proceed with short bursts of activity to maintain the spectators interest. Avoid long or complex sequences. During the demonstration, gauge the reaction of the audience to each segment of your presentation. If they respond well to a particular section, make a mental note to develop that more in future demonstrations. If they seem restless during a segment, consider revising or shortening it.

After the demonstration, make yourself available near the stage area. There will always be people who have questions or want information about your art or school. This is the time to actively promote your school to potential students. When the audience disperses, take some time to praise the performance of your students and give them feedback on their performance.

Sample Demonstration Plan

1. Spectators: Cub Scouts (100 boys)
2. Place: American School for the Deaf (outdoors)
3. Date: July 18th and August 1st
4. Time: 12:40 to 1:20 PM
5. Students: 25 children
6. Equipment: 50 1" boards
7. Content:
    a. introduction
    b. basic movements (5 min.)
    c. breaking (5 min.)
        side kick (3 people)
        axe kick/punch (5 people)
    d. form - poomse kicho (4 min.)
    e. breaking (6 min.)
        jumping back kick (5 people)
        knife hand (10 people)
    f. one step sparring (7 min.)
    g. form - poomse taegeuk sam jang (3 min.)
    h. self-defense (7 min.)
    i. group breaking - flying side kick (3 min.)
    j. closing comments and acknowledgments

Always take the time to give feedback to students who participate in demonstrations.

Equipment

There are many types of equipment that are used in martial arts training. Every piece of equipment has a specific function and purpose. Here is a brief summary of the most commonly used pieces of equipment.

Focus Mitts

Focus mitts are flat, padded gloves worn on the hands of the trainer. The student delivers kicks and hand strikes to the mitts to improve focus and power. The trainer should provide adequate resistance and the student should retract his attack quickly for power training. He also can vary the position and movement of the mitts to train for reflexes and timing.

Hand Held Targets

Hand held targets originated when Korean team players took the inner padding out of their sneakers to use as flexible targets to improve speed and accuracy. The targets used today are similarly shaped and come in single and double styles. They are excellent for speed and agility training, especially whipping techniques (roundhouse kick, hook kick, spinning whip kick) because they are flexible and the kick or strike can continue its path after striking the target.

Heavy Bags

Heavy bags come in many sizes from 30 to 150 pounds. They can be filled with a variety of substances including sand, stuffing, foam, and most recently, water. They are recommended for strength and power training for all linear (punching, side kick, back kick, front kick, jumping back kick, flying side kick) and angular (roundhouse kick, spinning crescent kick, spinning backfist, knifehand strikes) techniques. Avoid using whipping techniques (hook kick, spinning whip kick, axe kick) on the heavy bag to prevent joint injuries and dull movements.

For safety, start beginners on a less than full heavy bag. Proper density is one that allows penetration of the strike and does not cause the striker to rebound on impact. As the student improves power and strength move on to denser, heavier bags. Also, use proper equipment (bag gloves, tape, protection gear) to protect the skin and joints of the student.

Speed Bags

In general there are two kinds of speed bags - ceiling mounted and double ended. Ceiling mounted bags are primarily used to develop rhythm in hand skills by striking continuously in a specific pattern. Double ended bags are attached to the ceiling and floor by an elastic rope. They are used for developing rhythm, reflexes and agility in both hand and foot skills. Teach your competitors how to use speed bags to improve their sparring skills.

Makiwara

The makiwara is a traditional piece of equipment used to toughen the striking surfaces of the hands, feet, elbows shins and forearms. It is a solid piece of firmly padded material mounted on a post or block of wood. You can make a traditional makiwara by wrapping heavy rope around a 2" by 4" board and mounting it in the ground.

Modern makiwaras can be mounted on the wall or anchored in the ground. Standing makiwaras provide more flexibility when struck and are easier on the joints than wall mounted models. Conditioning through makiwara training should be gradual. Regular, moderate use of the makiwara produces long-term results without tissue or bone damage.

Weights

Weight training can be divided into two categories - lifting weights and personal weights. Lifting weights include dumbbells, barbells and all types of weight training machines. Weight lifting is an excellent aid to the martial arts when properly pursued. Weight lifting should focus on the specific muscles to be used. Emphasize high reps with light weights to maintain flexibility and agility.

Personal weights are weights worn by the athlete to strengthen specific areas of the body. They can be worn on the ankles and wrists. Weights should only be worn by athletes who are already in good physical condition. Never engage in activities that stress the joints when wearing weights. The best activities for personal weights are running, jumping rope, walking, and general conditioning exercises.

Jump Rope

Regular rope jumping improves endurance, timing and hand-eye/hand-foot coordination. It is highly recommended that competitors jump rope every day for at least the number of rounds they expect to fight in competition. The boredom of jumping can be lessened by alternating styles like single foot jumping, double foot jumping, crossovers, backwards jumping, double speed jumping, etc. The goal is to jump for as long as possible without interruption to improve concentration, rhythm, coordination and stamina.

Stretching Equipment

Stretching equipment comes in a variety of shapes and sizes. A wall mounted stretching bar is easy to construct and can be used for many activities to improve flexibility, balance, and basic skills. A stretching machine is also popular among students who need additional help in improving flexibility. Many machines have numbered gauges that provide instant feedback on how much improvement is taking place.

You can construct a simple stretching machine to improve flexibility and balance in kicking skills. Install a ceiling mounted pulley with a rope running through it. Place dowels at each end of the rope, one for the student to place his foot in and the other for him to hold and control the height of his foot. This device encourages correct technique in stretching because the student can adjust the height and angle of the stretch.

Training Weapons

Plastic, wooden or padded training weapons can be used in two ways. First, they can be used as a substitute for the real thing in teaching weapons skills to beginners. This ensures safety and gives the student more freedom to learn by experimentation. Second, use them to add realism to self-defense training. By using a simulated weapon, students get a realistic feel for the fine points of controlling the attacker and his weapon.

Video Tapes

Video tapes are an effective training aid for teaching new skills and perfecting complex movements. You can show students a training tape of the movements being performed correctly or you can tape the student's performance and analyze it. In either case, make use of slow motion and stop action features to pinpoint the critical details of each movement. After watching the tape, allow the student to practice and provide feedback according to what he saw on the taped performance. This helps the student compare his movement to his internalized picture of the ideal movement.

Protection Gear

The best way to ensure your students' safety is to require the use of protection gear for sparring. By the time students near the end of their basic training course, they have begun to participate in some form of contact training. Even if you teach only non-contact sparring, every student should have a full set of protection gear including shin/instep protectors, groin cup (males), gloves/arm guards, head gear and a mouthpiece. In addition you may require chest protectors if you practice controlled or full-contact sparring. All of this equipment is currently required by most tournaments and insurance companies, so it is a good idea to get your students in the habit of wearing it regularly.

Even if you are scrupulously careful, contact injuries can occur any time. Be prepared for this and give warnings to students who make excessive contact during sparring or partner activities. Eventually you may find that some people continue to make excessive contact in spite of your warnings. Suspend these people from partner drills until they gain better control of their body and mind. They are accidents waiting to happen but many accidents are preventable if you catch them in time.

Outdoor Training

By observing nature, we can discover the principles that govern martial arts training and the laws that govern humanity. From the ocean, we can learn generosity and depth of character. From the mountains, we can learn immovable strength and endurance. From the waterfall, we can learn the power of a group of tiny drops of water moving in unison. From the stars, we can learn a brilliant and unchanging temperament. And from the endless variety of trees, plants and animals, we can learn freedom, individuality and harmony.

Stop and think about the delicate balance that exists in our world. It is this balance that we, as martial artists, strive to achieve in our own lives. By studying the laws of nature, we attempt to create the ultimate mental and physical state of being. We hope to unlock the secrets of our own being that will free us from the limitations that we face as humans. We seek to run like tigers, fly like eagles, climb like monkeys, and capture the best that nature has to offer.

Why, then, do we spend most our training time indoors? Surely if we hope to emulate nature we have to go out and be a part of it. We have to see, smell, hear, taste, and touch its beauty and magnificence. We have to go to the mountain and ask it why it still stands after so many years. We have to study its foundation and scale its peak. We have to go to the ocean and look into its depths. We have to question why it is so deep that even humans, the most intelligent of species, cannot access all of its treasures.

Training outdoors is a way of attuning ourselves with nature. It is something every martial artist should experience. By observing the power and greatness of nature, we become inspired to reach new heights. With this in mind, I strongly recommend that you plan regular outdoor training or even a summer camp for your students. The warmth and beauty of spring and summer will invigorate your students mentally and physically.

If you decide to have a formal summer camp (or spring or fall camp) plan at least one year in advance. Choose a date and time that is convenient for the participants. Camps usually last for at least a weekend and often as long as a week. If you plan a year in advance, you can get the dates that you want at the facility of your choice. When you visit potential camp sites, check amenities such as sleeping facilities, water condition, bathrooms, showers, meal service, swimming areas, safety, cleanliness, privacy and natural beauty.

Once you have secured a facility, decide how many participants to accept and what the criteria for acceptance will be. You may have to place limitations based on age or rank depending on the material to be presented. Also, prepare necessary insurance and medical precautions in case of accidents.

If you have a large group, delegate authority to assistant instructors or group leaders. This leaves you free to perform administrative duties and handle crises as they arise. Encourage team spirit within small groups to make daily chores more enjoyable.

The activities that you plan for the camp can vary depending on your objectives. Try unusual activities that you cannot do in your school like sunrise training, morning and evening meditation, cross country running, water training, etc.

Remember to provide free periods so the participants can spend some uninterrupted time outdoors. Send them to the mountain and to the ocean. Provide them with the questions and let them seek out the answers.

The Leader

See the world as your self.
Have faith in the way
things are. Love the world
as your self; then you can
care for all things.
— Lao Tzu

Chapter 8
Qualities of a
Good Instructor

The qualifications to be a good instructor are many. Yet, in the teaching environment, the qualities of an instructor must be considered in human terms. In reality, all of the necessary qualifications can never be brought into perfect balance. Strength in one area compensates for weakness in another to form a solid personality. Consequently, there are many excellent teachers, all of whom have different personalities and teaching methods. What follows is a capsulated version of the qualities of a good instructor. Through it, find your weaknesses and strengths. Discover how to create the perfect balance of your skills.

To be a good instructor, have a **deep, well-rounded knowledge** of the art you teach. And, as an inseparable attribute, you need complete command of your skills and knowledge. Theory plus application equals mastery.

To be a good instructor, **understand teaching methodology.** Learn to transmit your knowledge to others in a clear, concise, interesting way. This will enable you to effectively share your ideas and abilities with the greatest number of people.

To be a good instructor, have a **sense of direction** for your school and your teaching. Develop the abilities to:

- ♦ see your teaching as a unified whole
- ♦ create new ideas
- ♦ sense and solve problems
- ♦ set goals in teaching
- ♦ set priorities in your life
- ♦ recognize problems in order of their importance
- ♦ analyze situations objectively
- ♦ clarify generalizations and obscurities
- ♦ plan a course of action with an open mind
- ♦ act with confidence according to your conclusions

A person who exhibits these qualities is often referred to as one who has a **vision for the future**.

To be a good instructor, **have enthusiasm and integrity**. Your ability to inspire your students to reach their goals depends on your ability to be inspired. Your students want to feel confident in placing their trust in you. They want to know that you are honest and sincere, that you keep your promises and that you have a passion for the martial arts in your heart.

To be a good instructor, **be friendly and considerate**. Be alert to the opinions of your students. Be sensitive to their feelings. Take care in what you say and how you say it. Be honest and fair to everyone, students and guests alike. Provide your students with a conflict-free atmosphere in which they can concentrate on learning.

To be a good instructor, **be decisive**. Understand what is important and reasonable and what is in the best interest of your students. Have the foresight to see the results of your decisions. The capacity and willingness to make good decisions are an integral part of success. Never be afraid to take a calculated risk.

To be a good instructor, **have an open mind**. Use common sense and see the reality of every situation. Don't be confined by prejudice or pride. Try new things at every opportunity. If you find a better alternative in your teaching or training, implement it. This is the only way to progress. If you follow the crowd, you may not become a leader. Through common sense, intellect, logical reasoning, research and an open mind you will discover ways to be a great leader.

To be a good instructor, **be healthy mentally and physically**. Have the mental strength to weather the storms that you will face. Have the physical strength to endure the rigors of your daily training. Eat well and lead a health conscious life style. Set an example for your students to follow. No matter what your age or ability, a strong body is a prerequisite for a healthy mind.

To be a good instructor, **be perceptive** regarding the needs of your students. Your teaching exists for the benefit of the students. Without them, you cannot be an instructor. Consider your students in every decision.

Finally, to be a good instructor, **have faith** in what you are doing. Know that you are doing the greatest job in the world by teaching, guiding, and helping others. Your positive attitude will be contagious. The better the quality of your teaching, the better your students will become. The greater your students are, the greater your school will be. Your leadership will change your students. What your students become will change the world around them. When you unselfishly help your students, they become inspired to help others. This can start an endless chain of fellowship and goodwill. Perhaps hundreds of years from now, the world will be a better place because of the efforts we are making today.

As an instructor you are both a pioneer for the future and a keeper of the wisdom of the past.

Do not seek to follow in the footsteps of the men of old; seek what they sought.

– Basho

Glossary

Action Visualization - creating a mental picture to aid in learning or improving individual skills

Aerobic - Requiring the presence of oxygen

Anaerobic - pertaining to the absence of oxygen

Counter Attack - a defensive blow delivered in response to the opponent's attack

Curriculum - the course of study of a particular school or teaching system

Fast Twitch Muscle Fibers - the fibers of each muscle that initiate and control explosive movements

Feedback - knowledge of the results of behavior intended to modify or influence the behavior.

Form - a prearranged series of offensive and defensive movements

Fundamental Physical Training - activities that help the athlete reach his optimal physical condition

Hyung - *see* Form

Initiative Attack - an offensive attempt to score on or damage the opponent

Isometric Exercise - any exercise that aims to strengthen specific muscles by pitting one or more muscles against each other or against an immovable object

Joasun - *see* Zazen

Joplin Plan - Grouping students according to ability level without regard for age

Kata - *see* Form

Kiai - an explosive exhalation of air that produces a sharp sound

Kihap - *see* Kiai

Lesson Plan - a set of objectives and a means to implement the objectives for a single class

Makiwara - flat or padded striking surface used to condition parts of the body used in martial arts

Metabolism - the sum of physical and chemical processes in the human body through which energy is produced

Negative Transfer - a situation in which prior learning interferes with subsequent learning

Performance Assessment - a five step method used to evaluate and improve skills

Plateau - a period of little or no apparent progress in learning

Poomse- *See* Form

Prearranged Sparring - a drill in which two opponents attack and defend using previously defined techniques

Positive Transfer - a situation in which prior learning aids subsequent learning

Preventive Discipline - actions taken to maintain stability and order in the learning environment

Reaction Visualization - creating a mental picture to improve interactive skills

Regrouping - structuring class according to student's age and ability in a single subject

Reinforcement - actions or words intended to strengthen a behavior through positive or negative means.

Remedial Discipline - actions taken to eliminate undesirable behavior and return the student to the desired course

Sensory Register - the area of the brain that filters incoming stimulus and controls attention.

Sport Specific Training - conditioning of the muscles predominantly used in the sport in which the athlete engages

Target Visualization - creating a mental image of a target to be attacked

Technical Practice - activities designed to improve the skills needed to perform at the optimal level in a sport

Zazen - seated meditation

Zen - a practice in which the student attempts to attain enlightenment through the most direct means possible

Zero Transfer - a situation in which prior learning has no effect on subsequent learning

BONUS SECTION

⌘

Launching a Martial Arts School

Launching a Martial Arts School

Starting a new martial arts school is a demanding and exciting venture. Through opening your own school, you gain the opportunity to enrich the lives of hundreds or even thousands of students. You also take on the burden of supporting yourself through running your own business.

Before you make the decision to open a commercial martial arts school, there are several areas you must contemplate, including your financial considerations and the details of finding a location, negotiating a lease, etc. This preparation is all part of the *initiation phase*. After the initiation phase, you enter the *launching phase* in which you furnish the school, prepare your administrative system and begin advertising. Once the school is up and running, you enter the final start-up phase which is the *establishment phase*. During this period, you establish your schedule, register new students and setup student and curriculum tracking methods that will be the backbone of your school management.

PHASE 1: INITIATION PHASE

A. Assessing your start-up costs

The first thing you need to do is to assess how much money you have available to invest versus how much money you need to invest during the initiation and launching phases. During the first two phases of starting the school, you will not make any money, so you have to set aside enough money to carry you through to Phase 3. To calculate your start-up costs, fill in the work sheet on the following page.

Start-up work sheet

1. Business license   _____
2. Insurance (liability/contents)   _____
3. Sales tax application(s)   _____
4. Other tax application(s)   _____
5. Business checks (500)   _____
6. Security deposit   _____
7. First month rent   _____
8. Deposit for utilities   _____
9. Yellow pages ad (first month)   _____
10. Grand opening flyers   _____
11. Brochures   _____
12. Contracts   _____
13. Business cards   _____
14. Uniforms (to sell to students)   _____
15. Telephone   _____
16. Answering machine   _____
17. Chairs for waiting area   _____
18. Mats and/or rugs   _____
19. Targets/bags   _____
20. Safety equipment   _____
21. Mirrors   _____
22. Desk and chair   _____
23. Cleaning supplies   _____
24. File cabinet   _____
25. Flags   _____
26. Frames for certificates   _____
27. Misc. Decorations   _____
28. Outside Sign   _____
29. Window Signs   _____
30. 2 clocks   _____
31. First aid kit   _____
32. Wastebaskets   _____
33. Accounting/recording supplies   _____
34. Other   _____

Total Projected Start-up cost   _____

Filling out the start-up work sheet: step-by-step

1. Contact city hall to find out what type of paperwork you must file and how much it costs.

2. Liability insurance is essential, no matter how costly it is. Fire/theft insurance is optional depending on how much money you have invested in the contents of the school. If you have a small investment, you can always add contents coverage later.

3. Contact your state, county and/or city tax offices for the cost of filing.

4. Contact your accountant for filing costs of any other necessary tax forms.

5. Call your bank to find out the least expensive set of checks you can order for a business. 500 is enough to get you started.

6 & 7. Your landlord may require a security deposit and/or the first month's rent before you can move in.

8. Most utilities companies require one to two months deposit to turn on service. Contact the utility companies for costs.

9. You may have to pay the first month's yellow pages ad in advance, depending on the deadlines in your area. Contact the yellow pages publisher for the rates and deadlines.

10-13. Get bids from local print shops for these items. You can make them on your copier, but a print shop lends a professional touch for only a few dollars more.

15-17, 22-24, 26 & 33. Shop around at your local department stores for the best prices.

18. This may or may not be an expense depending on the condition of the space you are renting and the type of art you teach.

14, 19, 20 & 25. Obtain wholesale information from the local or national martial arts suppliers to project these costs. Although you should order only the minimum amount necessary to get you started, you usually have to make a significant initial purchase to establish wholesale status with these companies.

21. When soliciting prices for mirrors, don't forget installation costs. They must be professionally installed.

27. This item is optional depending on how much extra money you have to spend.

28. As with the mirrors, signs often have to be installed professionally and your landlord or town may have strict regulations regarding size, color, etc. Confirm these requirements before you order your sign.

29. You can make brightly colored signs from poster paper or have banners printed at the local sign shop.

30. Plan on one clock for the training area and one for your office.

31. A first aid kit should include band aids, antibacterial ointment and spray, ice packs, gauze, athletic tape (1/2 " and 1"), smelling salts, pain relief tablets and scissors at the very least.

32. Provide wastebaskets in both locker rooms, both bathrooms, your office and the waiting area.

34. Use this space for any expenses not included above.

The above list is a general list of things common to most new schools. Depending on your situation, you may have additional needs. For example, if the landlord is not providing renovations, you have to budget money for paint, trash removal, construction work, etc. If you are starting a professional kickboxing gym, you have to purchase additional equipment, such as a competition ring and heavy bags.

Once you have completed your start-up list, you need to estimate your monthly expenses. Use the following work sheet to do this.

Monthly expense work sheet

1. Rent   _____

2. Telephone   _____

3. Utilities   _____

4. Yellow pages   _____

5. Other advertising   _____

6. Merchandise   _____

7. Bank service charges   _____

8. Misc supplies   _____

9. other   _____

                                     _____

                                     _____

Total estimated expenses   _____

Filling out the monthly expense work sheet: step-by-step

1. You should have an exact figure or at least a maximum allowance for this category.

2. Basic business rate plus long distance calls. Once you establish your school, you should invest in two telephone lines or call waiting to take additional calls while you are on the line.

3. Depending on your lease this could include oil/gas heat, electricity, water, trash removal, janitorial, snow removal/landscaping. If you have negotiated a good lease, at least some of these will be included.

4 & 5. Advertising will consume 10 to 30 percent of initial monthly income, do not under-budget.

6. This figure depends on the number of students you have and how much merchandise you sell. Make a rough estimate of $5 - $10 per student per month.

7. Most banks charge service fees on business accounts. Contact your bank for a list of applicable charges and rates.

8. You will run out of various supplies, office and cleaning regularly. Budget $50 - $100 per month for these miscellaneous expenses. Join a "warehouse club" to save money on supplies by purchasing in bulk.

9. Include anything not specified above.

Before you prepare to open your school, you should have saved at *least your start-up expenses plus the first two months expenses.* This is a minimum figure and anything you have set aside above this amount will be additional security for you. If you do not have at least your start-up plus first two months on hand, you are probably not ready to launch your own school yet. Set a savings goal and establish a regular savings plan until you reach that goal. In the mean time, you can work on planning your curriculum, designing advertisements, studying further, and generally preparing yourself for the time when you are ready to begin your new venture.

B. Setting your tuition rates

Once you have established your monthly expenses, you have a basis for setting your monthly tuition rates. There are two basic methods for setting rates:

1. **Market dependent** - Market dependent rates are set based on what others in your area are charging. You can choose to meet or beat local prices, depending on your income needs. If you are in a less expensive location than your competition, you will definitely need to beat their rates. Less expensive usually means less desirable, meaning you have to give people a reason to put aside the inconvenience of coming to your location instead of going to the school in the mall or shopping center. If you have a better location than the competition, you should meet their prices and emphasize more value for the money.

2. **Break even** - Your break even point is the point at which you can cover you monthly expenses and your salary with the tuition income from your students. There are two ways to find your break even point:

Formula A

Add your estimated expenses plus your salary and divide by the number of students you expect to average each month in your first year in business. The figure you get will be the minimum monthly tuition fee you must charge. For example, if your monthly expenses including salary are $3000.00 and you expect to have 50 students average, you need to charge $60.00 per month per student average. This method is based on knowing how many students you expect to average in your first year of business.

Formula A: $$\frac{\text{expenses} + \text{salary}}{\text{\# students}} = \text{Break even monthly rate}$$

Example A: $$\frac{\$3000.00}{50 \text{ students}} = \$60.00 \text{ per month}$$

Formula B

If you have an idea of what you want to charge, but do not know how many students you will need to cover expenses at that rate, add your *expenses and salary and divide by the average monthly rate to get the number of students you need to break even.* For example, if you want to charge $50.00 a month and have $3000.00 in expenses and salary, you will need to average 60 students a month to break even.

Formula B: $$\frac{expenses + salary}{monthly\ rate} = Break\ even\ students$$

Example B: $$\frac{\$3000.00}{\$50.00} = 60\ students$$

When you set your rates, you have to accept the fact that it will be a few months before your reach your break even goal, no matter how modest it is. To account for this, you have base your estimates on the average number of students you expect to have at the end of one year.

Once you have determined your average monthly rate, you need to develop a sliding scale that allows discounts for longer term contracts. If you decide to charge $50.00 a month and let everyone pay $50.00 at the beginning of each month, they have no incentive sign up for more than one month at time. However, if you charge $55.00 per month for monthly payers and $45.00 per month for students who are willing to commit to one year, everyone has a good incentive to make a long-term commitment to your school, both financially and mentally. Most students opt for the longer term rate if your teaching is good and your business practices are sound. Although you make slightly less than your projected average monthly rate, you make up the difference in the long run by keeping more students for a longer time.

Setting tuition rates case study:

1. Determine which formula to use
    a. Market Dependent
    b. Break Even Formula A
    c. Break Even Formula B
2. Calculate your base monthly rate
3. Develop a sliding scale
4. Plan special discounts or offers

Example

1. Using Break Even Formula A:

2. $$\frac{\$1200 \text{ salary} + \$1950 \text{ expenses}}{70 \text{ students}} = \frac{3150}{70} = \$45.00$$

3. Sliding Scale:

Monthly	$50.00 per month
6 months	$45.00 per month
1 year	$40.00 per month

4. Discounts: 1 year paid in full earns a free uniform
    6 months paid in full earns a free T-shirt
    Family rate: 1st person full price, others 50% off

Based on the base tuition rate, you can offer special discounts, bonuses for payment in full on long-term contracts and special seasonal offers. Since markets differ from state to state, you can start with ideas that are popular with your local competitors and develop your own variations or new ideas as you experiment. As you progress, you will find ideas that work brilliantly as well as those that fail miserably. Do not be afraid of the failures, they are part of the learning process and anyone who has ever succeeded in business has experienced their fair share.

C. Finding a Location

Once you have established that your business plan is feasible and you have set your financial guidelines, you begin your search for a location. There are three options for a martial arts school location:

1. YMCA/YWCA/Recreation Program/Community Center

If you have only *a small amount of money to invest*, consider a YMCA, YWCA, recreation program or community center. They rent out their gyms and public rooms for a small fee and may even advertise for you. If you are especially lucky, you can find a program where you give the sponsoring organization a percentage of your tuition. If you have only a few students or cannot afford a fixed rent, this is ideal.

2. Industrial/secondary location

If you can afford *a modest rent*, you need to look for a secondary location such as an industrial park, warehouse, second floor, back entrance or off the main road type location. Due to the low visibility/low traffic, the rent is cheaper. Because the rent is cheaper, you can afford to charge less for lessons, but you have to spend more time and effort for promotion and advertising. For the beginning instructor with much time and energy, this is a profitable trade off.

3. Prime retail

Prime retail space is for those who are *experienced enough or well-financed* enough to afford a high rent/high traffic location such as a mall.

Although the front end costs are higher, the benefits of a high traffic location more than pay for themselves in the long run. Because your break even numbers are significantly higher than in the first two locations, the prime retail location is a good choice if you already have a student base or if you have a lot of investment money set aside.

When selecting a location, you have to consider the local zoning codes. The real estate representative for the space or the zoning commissioner can help you learn if you can legally operate a school in the chosen space. *Always confirm the zoning feasibility before you begin to negotiate the lease.*

D. Negotiating the Lease

Negotiating a lease is one of the biggest tasks you undertake in opening your school and you should retain the services of a lawyer to look out for your interests. In general, you should look for a lease that includes one month rent-free to move in and setup, a small security deposit, utilities/ maintenance included and renovations to suit your needs. Obviously you must pay more for an all-inclusive lease, but if times are tough or the building has been empty for a few months, you can use these bonuses as bargaining chips. Once you have done the early   negotiations, turn the lease over to your lawyer for a professional opinion on any changes that may need to be made to protect your rights as a tenant.

E. Establishing your Business as a Legal Entity

There are several important steps you must take to legally establish and protect your new business. Once you have secured a lease, you must file the appropriate federal and local tax forms including an application for a Federal Employer I.D. number (which you need to apply for a business checking account) and necessary sales tax forms (state, county, city as required). You can expect to pay a small fee with each application. The advice of a professional accountant is required at this stage to be certain you are complying with all applicable tax laws.

Once you have obtained your tax i.d. numbers, you can apply for a business checking account at your local bank. Select a generic set of checks and order 500 to 1000 to get you started. Business checking is more expensive than a personal account, due to service charges and higher per check fees. Ask for a list of all charges you may incur as well as the cost of the checks you have selected. Shop around for the lowest rates if possible.

At this time, you will also have to apply for a business license or trade name. To find out what your city or town requires, visit the clerk at city hall and request all of the forms necessary for starting a new business. There is a small fee for registering your business with the town.

Once you have established your business as a legal entity, you need to apply for liability insurance. Although you will require every student to sign a liability waiver, you are not fully protected by the waiver. By purchasing liability insurance, you have a safety net. Additionally most landlords will require at least $1,000,000.00 in liability insurance, with their name included on the policy.

The insurance company requires you to provide a copy of the liability waiver your students are required to sign. They will not provide coverage unless you provide proof that all students must sign a valid liability waiver. Your attorney can provide you with a standard liability waiver to include in your contract.

Establishing your Business Checklist

1. Find a location
2. Confirm zoning feasibility
3. Negotiate the lease
4. Register your business with the city
5. Apply for state, local and federal tax permits
6. Open a business checking account
7. Apply for liability insurance

PHASE 2: LAUNCHING PHASE

A. Advertising and Promotion

The key to launching your new school is generating interest among potential students. Obviously this is a very specific market that you must locate and target effectively. You are not aiming to promote your school to the entire population in the town. You are aiming for a few specific groups of people and your advertising and promotion should reflect this.

Assume you are interested in teaching mainly children in the six to twelve age group. First list all the places these children gather: boy/girl scouts, elementary school, YMCA, recreations centers, youth sports leagues, etc. These are all excellent places to approach to distribute free lesson coupons, lessons as prizes, free demonstrations, team sponsorship and any other effort that will make your school visible to the youngsters. Additionally consider how you can reach their parents: local newspaper, direct mail, coupon shoppers, flyers in the supermarket or library, word of mouth, PTA/PTO, etc.

Once you identify your primary market(s), you can develop advertising and promotional plans accordingly. The following are some cost effective ways to generate interest in your new school:

1. Yellow pages ad

You must have a yellow pages advertisement. This is not a place to skimp or save money. The number one source of students for an established school is the yellow pages. The reason for this? Imagine you need to find a plumber, painter, accountant, dance school or other service in your area. If you do not know of anyone off hand, you probably open the telephone directory and start calling businesses, beginning with the largest or most impressive ads first. People who see your yellow pages ad are already interested and need only chose who to learn from.

2. Grand opening flyers

Grand opening flyers can be very cost effective. Design a catchy black and white ad and have it photocopied on colored paper. Keep it simple and make an irresistible, limited time offer. Then distribute the flyers at demonstrations, on public bulletin boards, in parking lots, to neighborhood homes (remember it is illegal to place any non-stamped items in mail boxes), at friends' businesses, etc. This will be your second greatest source of new students when you start.

3. News release

A news release detailing the opening of your school, your credentials and the benefits your school offers to the community should be sent to all of the local newspapers. Make it exciting and newsworthy and include two black and white photos, an action shot of yourself and one of the front of your school. (For more information on new releases and publicity, see the special report available from Turtle Press, "Publicity for the Martial Arts School".)

4. Newspaper ads

New instructors are often disappointed by the response they receive from newspaper ads. There are several reasons for this. Sometimes the ad is too small, poorly done or too commonplace to attract attention. More likely, the instructor has overestimated the pull of newspaper. The nature of a print ad is fleeting. It has one chance to grab the attention of a busy reader and the chance that the reader just happened to be thinking about taking martial arts lessons (yet has not looked into any schools) is rather slim. Experiment with different ads and media.

Certain types of medium have more potential students than others. Two key markets are the "shopper" newspaper and the "alternative" magazine or newspaper. When you find something that works, stick with it relentlessly. In the author's personal experience, one local newspaper drew little response with a few different ads while another paper continues to draw responses after four years of running the same ad every other week.

5. Coupons/mailers

After you open for business you will be approached by a myriad of media representatives who offer to put your ad on everything from cash register tapes to coupons to calendars. Generally the ad cost for these local companies is small and worth a try at least once. Do not be afraid to experiment with small ads in a variety of places. The more often people in your community see your name, the more familiar you become. If they decide to take up the martial arts in the future, your school name may come to mind first.

6. Student incentives

Once you have some students, you can establish an incentive program for referrals. Offer a small incentive, such as a uniform, gear or gift certificate for each student who refers a new student. You may also want to provide a special offer for the new student as well. If your students can say to their friends or family members, "I just started learning martial arts at _____ and it's great. In fact if you want to come down and try out a class with me you'll get a free uniform when you sign up.", they will have that much more incentive to brag about how great your school is. If you teach well and have a sizable student base, referrals will become your best source of new students.

Target marketing work sheet
(use one work sheet for each target market)

1. My target market is:_____

2. These potential students can be reached through:

_____

_____

3. My yellow pages ad will emphasize:

_____

_____

4. I will distribute flyers to:

_____

5. I will send press releases to:

_____

6. I will advertise in:

_____

7. I will use coupons/direct mail through:

_____

8. I will offer the following student incentives:

_____

B. Creating your Business Image

When prospective students walk into your school, you want to project a specific image to them. For a martial arts school, the best image is one of professionalism, seriousness and concern for their or their child's well-being. One of the best ways to establish a professional image is to create a consistent feeling throughout all of your contacts with the prospective student.

The first contact will probably be with your advertising, which we discussed above. After you design your ads, try to maintain a consistent style throughout all forms of media. Use a consistent typeface for your school name as well as a logo and slogan. Based on this image, you can develop supporting materials including business cards, brochures, contracts, uniforms, school rules and a schedule.

Business cards

Business cards with your name, logo or slogan, school name, address and telephone number lend an air of professionalism to your business. However, the business card is meant to be a way of letting contacts remember you, not mini-advertisement for your school. Keep your card simple and professional.

Brochure

Many people will drop by your school to pick up written information about your school, art, instructors, etc. You can prepare a simple, tri-fold brochure with black ink on colored paper. Include a brief history/summary of the art you teach, highlights of your credentials, benefits of martial arts for children and adults, your teaching philosophy, class schedule, special beginner program offer/trial lesson offer, answers to commonly asked questions and your school name, address, phone. Make the brochure exciting and credible. Provide plenty of facts and positive reassurances for the prospective student.

Contracts

A contract is essential to running a professional school. You will see at least one school in every community that advertises "no contracts." They are generally small schools or community programs who try to draw people who are afraid of making a commitment. A contract is simply a commitment made by both you and the student. You commit to hold classes regularly and teach professionally for the duration of the contract, while the student agrees to come to class regularly and pay the specified tuition for the specified period.

Present it to the student as an enrollment agreement and mention that your insurance company requires everyone to fill out and sign the liability waiver included at the bottom. If you present the contract as a mere formality after the student has decided to sign-up ("let's just fill out the paperwork and get you into a class"), he or she will be happy to oblige. Be sure to have your contract reviewed by a lawyer who can verify that you are complying with state and federal laws.

School rules

Every school should have a set of rules that are clearly posted in the school as well as provided to each student at enrollment. This serves several purposes: your insurance company will require it, you can enforce the rules without question from the students, the students have a set of guidelines for their behavior in the school setting and you can protect yourself against potentially harmful actions by disgruntled students. The school rules should include *etiquette rules* (bowing, hygiene), *class rules* (contact allowed, gear required), and *personal conduct rules* (no foul language, no gum in class).

Uniforms

Once you establish your school, you can custom print uniforms, T-shirts, patches, bags, etc. with your school logo. Your students will proudly wear/ use these items both in and out of class, showing off your school name and image to their friends and family. This is one of the best ways of building your school image.

Furnishing your School

Before you begin classes, you must purchase furnishings, both decorative and functional. The following is breakdown of necessary purchases by category:

1. **Office**

    a. Desk
    b. 1 chair for you and 2 for visitors
    c. Telephone
    d. Answering machine
    e. 2 or 4 drawer file cabinet
    f. Your certificates, diplomas, awards
    g. Frames for certificates and diplomas
    h. Clock
    i. Wastebasket
    j. Accounting and record keeping supplies

2. **Training area**

    a. Mats and/or rug (depends on your style)
    b. Mirrors on one or two walls
    c. Flags (country or association of martial art)
    d. Appropriate artwork/calligraphy
    e. Safety equipment
    f. Targets and/or heavy bag
    g. Action pictures of yourself/students
    h. First aid kit
    i. Clock

3. **Entrance/waiting area**

    a. Chairs for visitors
    b. News articles about school
    c. Bulletin board for announcements
    d. Action pictures of yourself and students

e. Appropriate artwork
f. Coat/shoes room with hooks and shelves
g. Children's play corner with quiet toys
h. trophies
i. wastebasket

4. Locker rooms

a. Chairs/bench
b. Hooks/shelves
c. Lockers (optional)
d. wastebasket

5. Maintenance closet

a. Cleaning supplies
b. Wet and dry mop
c. Vacuum cleaner and broom

6. Building front

a. Building sign
b. Window signs

This list includes the most basic necessities. As you proceed, you may discover necessities unique to your school and students. When selecting furnishings, expand on the image of your school that you developed in your advertising and brochures. Some schools are very traditional with lots of oriental artwork and polished hardwood floors. Others are more functional with mats and plenty of exercise equipment. Some are very businesslike with sleek furnishings and plenty of office space. And some are just barebones, a floor and four walls.

All these types of schools are successful in their own way. Discover the best fit for you and then draw students who agree with your style and philosophy. You cannot be everything to everyone, nor should you try. Define your style and believe in it. Soon you will find many   like-minded people who want to learn from you.

PHASE 3:
ESTABLISHMENT PHASE

A. Planning a Class Schedule

Before you can register any students, you have set up a class schedule. Classes should be divided first by age then by rank. The ideal age groups are:

Peewee	4 - 7 years old
Junior	8 - 12 years old
Teen	13 - 17 years old
Adult	18 - 35 years old
Executive	36 + years old

However, most schools do not have the students to fill this many classes or the instructors to teach them. At a minimum you should have three classes: Peewee (4-7), Junior (8-12), and Adult (13 +). Once teenagers reach high school age they prefer to be treated as adults and respond much better in the adult class than in the children classes.

Occasionally, younger children may have schedule conflicts, resulting in the need to place them in the adult class. This can work if you do not let the children distract the adults and if you occasionally give the children some special fun activities to hold their interest. In general, children who train in the adult classes become more serious and technically superior to those who attend children's classes.

Once you have divided the students into age groups, divide them by belt. The ideal belt structure is one class for each two or three belt levels. For example:

Beginner	First 3 belt levels
Intermediate	Middle 3 belt levels
Advanced	Remaining belts up to black
Black Belt class	All level black belts

When you start your school you will probably have only a beginner children's class and a beginner adult class. As the students progress in level, add classes accordingly. A small school can get by with a beginner and advanced class for each age group. If your school grows beyond 200 students, you will need to add a black belt class and perhaps another level to keep students interested and hold down the class numbers.

Another consideration in scheduling classes is a morning or lunch time class for people with unconventional schedules. A morning class accommodates people who work second or third shift and are either sleeping or working during evening class hours. A lunch time class accommodates people who work during the day and have school or another event in the evening. Both classes are optional and usually remain small, no matter how big your other classes grow.

Sample class schedule: Small to medium sized school

Monday and Wednesday	5:30 to 6:30 PM	Peewee beginners
Monday and Wednesday	7:00 to 8:00 PM	Adult beginners
Tuesday and Thursday	5:30 to 6:30 PM	Junior beginners
Tuesday and Thursday	7:00 to 8:00 PM	Intermediate belts
Saturday	10:00 to 11:00 AM	Juniors (all)
Saturday	11:30 to 12:30 PM	Adults (all)

B. Advance Registration

At this point you should be finishing the furnishing of the school, have the schedule set, the advertisements placed, the flyers distributed, the brochures and contracts ready and be generally ready to handle inquiries from potential students. This is the time when everything is coming together, but not quite ready for the grand opening. Now is the time to register students through an advance registration program.

About two weeks before you are ready to open, advertise for advance registration for classes. Create ads with the theme of "register now for classes starting on xxxxx date." Encourage people to call or make an appointment to stop by and register.

When you receive inquiries, explain that classes are starting on xxxxx date and that you are currently reserving places for new students as class numbers are limited on a first come/first serve basis. Ask the prospective student to stop by at an agreed upon time to fill out a registration form (contract) and pick up their official uniform. Now is the time to create urgency, for example, "Can you stop by Saturday morning. I have a lot of people coming by this weekend and I'm afraid classes may be full by Monday."

Callers will have many questions, some serious and some not. You do not need to stick to a preset script or use a hard sell over the phone.

C. Professional Telephone Tips

1. Answer the phone politely and professionally.

2. Have a professional message on your answering machine.

3. Return all messages the same day if possible.

4. If you cannot reach the caller, leave a brief message to let them know that you at least tried to reach them. Offer to call back at a convenient time.

5. Learn the caller's needs first. Who are the lessons for? Are you a beginner? When is the best time to come to class? What type of classes are you interested in? (if you offer a choice)

6. Based on this information, inform the caller of the best class schedule and the price of your basic course.

7. Make an appointment to register for classes or take a trial lesson.

8. Give the caller directions, a contact name and what, if anything, to bring.

9. Be sincere and friendly.

10. Do not hard sell or be evasive. If the caller does not trust you, you will never hear from them again.

11. Honestly address any fears or misconceptions the caller expresses or implies. (i.e. Isn't Karate violent? Won't my son hit kids at school? Aren't I too old for this? Can women do this too?)

12. Admit when you cannot offer what the caller is looking for. (i.e. They want tai chi but you teach kickboxing or vice versa) Perhaps they are not interested in kickboxing, but their teenage son might be. Always leave a door open.

13. Set limits on what information you are willing to provide over the telephone. This generally includes an appropriate schedule, a basic course price, directions and addressing any fears/misconceptions of the caller. If the student wants to discuss in depth questions about your teaching philosophy, comparisons of styles, your entire tuition rate structure, testing requirements, etc. suggest that he or she make an appointment for an interview, tour of the school and a trial lesson. These questions cannot be properly addressed over the telephone.

14. Do not waste time with nuisance callers. These are the people who call and ask questions for ten minutes then say thank you and hang up, never

to be heard from again. After a few months in business, you will be able to identify them early in the conversation. The best way to handle them is to say, "I have to go to class now, but if you would like to make an appointment to come down and talk further I would be happy to schedule you for later in the week." At this point, most nuisance callers will say they are too busy to stop by but will get back to you.

15. Do not dismiss calls from youngsters. Many parents tell their children to call and get prices if they want to learn. If the child sounds old enough to write down the information accurately, provide him with a simple price and time schedule then ask him to stop by with his parents for a trial lesson. You may be surprised at the number of these children who join if you treat them with patience and respect.

16. Take the initiative without being pushy or aggressive. Try to direct the conversation toward your chosen objective while still answering the concerns of the caller. This technique takes practice and patience, but pays off far better then a mechanical scripted performance.

17. Respond to hostility with polite detachment. Never get drawn into a fight with a caller. If you cannot defuse the caller's hostility or aggression, politely excuse yourself by feigning an unexpected visitor or a pressing appointment.

D. Recruiting Students from Auxiliary Programs

If you teach at a YMCA or recreation program, this is the best source for new students when you open your school. At the end of the current session, pass out flyers for your new school or make an announcement that all program students will have a special rate if they sign up within 2 weeks. These students are already interested in learning, are familiar with you and have made a significant physical and mental investment in their training. They are prime candidates for your school.

E. Registering the student

There are two ways of registering students for classes. If the student has already decided to sign-up, usually because they know you or have heard about your school from a friend, simply have them fill out the paperwork and schedule their first class.

If they are uncertain, schedule a trial lesson. Trial lessons should always be free and all beginners are entitled to one, provided they are of legal adult age or have a parent's permission. You can give trial lessons privately or have the student join the group class. In either case, make the lesson simple, interesting and fun. Be encouraging but honest. If the student is awkward or uncoordinated, find something positive to say about even the most minor aspect of their performance.

Generally children respond best in group trial classes because they are very flexible and make friends easily. If the child is shy, start with a private lesson and join the group when the child is ready. Most adults respond to a private or group lesson equally well and the group lesson is the most efficient for you. If you give a private trial lesson, keep it short, 15 to 25 minutes, so the student does not become tired or bored. When he or she is beginning to learn something and looks confident, it is time to end the trial lesson and sign him or her up.

F. Student Tracking

To run a successful, professional school, you need to keep track of certain key elements of your day to day activities, as well as the activities of your students. There are eleven basic record keeping forms that you should maintain.

A. Student Records:

1. **Student phone list.** The student phone list is simply a master list of all of your active students' names and telephone numbers. You can keep this list in a notebook, adding new names as new students join, and crossing

out names as students become inactive. Depending on your dropout rate, you must occasionally begin a new list, eliminating students who quit and consolidating active students. If you have a computer, this list can easily be kept and updated in a word processor file. Use this list to contact students who have missed classes or as a quick reference when you need to telephone a student or parent.

2. **Renewal list.** This is a list of the students up for renewal in the coming weeks. Every two weeks, compile a list of students whose contract is due to expire in the next fourteen days. List their name, telephone number and current contract length. Use this list to contact students to renew their membership.

3. **Student background record.** This is a record form containing the background information for each student. Background information includes name, address, telephone number, age, birth date, social security number, date of entrance, date of renewal, promotion records, competition records, event participation records, awards, and other important information. By filing all of this information on a single form, you have handy reference for each student. Keep the records in alphabetical order in a file cabinet or 3 ring binder and regularly remove inactive students.

4. **Attendance records**. Each student should have an attendance tracking record and should sign-in for every class he or she attends. Once a week, go through the attendance records and contact every student who is missing classes or has irregular attendance for the previous two weeks. Attendance records designed specifically for martial arts schools can be purchased from Turtle Press (PO Box 290206, Wethersfield CT 06129-0206) for a small fee.

B. Teaching Records

5. **Lesson Plans.** You should have a lesson plan made up for every class before you set foot in the training hall. Consistent lesson plans are essential for organized, progressive classes. Keep your lesson plans for each class (i.e. beginner, children, etc.) together in a notebook or binder, so you

can track the progress of the class and plan future classes accordingly.

6. **Appointment calendar.** A desk calendar or appointment book is essential for organizing your non-class time. Keep your calendar at your desk and use it to record trial lessons, new student appointments, student interviews, business meetings, etc. Always keep all of your appointments on one calendar to avoid scheduling conflicting appointments.

C. Financial Records

7. **Currently due tuition list.** This is a list of all tuition payments due in the coming weeks. Compile this list from your student contracts and use it to create your overdue lists by marking off payments as they are made.

8. **Overdue tuition list.** This is the list of tuition that is past due, usually by a few days or more. Use this list to contact and remind students who are past due. Most students will pay all or at lest a portion of the delinquent payment after your first reminder.

9. **Income ledger.** Use this list to record all income from tuition, merchandise, testing, seminars, and sales tax.

10. **Expense ledger.** Use this list to record all business related expenses for tax records. Remember to keep receipts and other records to prove the expense was business related.

11. **Student receipt book**. Keep a receipt book handy to issue receipts for payments and purchases made by students. This is especially important for purchases made in cash, providing a record of the transaction for both you and the student.

The record forms listed above are the backbone of an effective record keeping system and you may find other records that are useful or necessary during your work.

Index

About the Author

Sang H. Kim is an internationally acclaimed authority on teaching martial arts, author of seven martial arts books and star of over forty instructional video tapes. Dr. Kim travels extensively throughout the world presenting martial arts seminars and motivational lectures. He continues to actively pursue his martial arts training, holding master rankings in taekwondo, hapkido, junsado and kumdo.

Additional books Available from Turtle Press

Combat Strategy
The Art of Harmony
A Guide to Rape Awareness and Prevention
Total MindBody Training
1,001 Ways to Motivate Yourself and Others
Ultimate Fitness through Martial Arts
Taekwondo Kyorugi: Olympic Style Sparring
Launching a Martial Arts School
Advanced Teaching Report
Hosting a Martial Art Tournament
100 Lost Cost Marketing Ideas for the Martial Arts School
A Part of the Ribbon: A Time Travel Adventure
The Martial Arts Training Diary
Neng Da: Super Punches
50 Drills for the Martial Arts Instructor

For more information:

Turtle Press
PO Box 290206
Wethersfield CT 06129-206
1-800-77-TURTL
e-mail: sales@turtlepress.com
http://www.turtlepress.com